9/99

**Eric Davis, James Martin,**

**and Randy Holcomb, with**

**Luchina Fisher**

A Seth Godin Production
Simon & Schuster

# The Slick Boys

A Ten-Point Plan to Rescue
Your Community by Three
Chicago Cops Who Are
Making It Happen

SIMON & SCHUSTER

Rockefeller Center

1230 Avenue of the Americas

New York, NY 10020

Copyright © 1998 by Eric Davis, Randy Holcomb, James Martin, Glenn Merrill, and
Steven B. Muslin

Designed by Karolina Harris

Manufactured in the United States of America

10 9 8 7 6 5 4 3 2 1

Library of Congress Cataloging-in-Publication Data

The Slick Boys : a ten-point plan to rescue your community by three Chicago cops who are
making it happen / Eric Davis ... [et al.].

        p.  cm.

    Includes index.

        1. Police—Illinois—Chicago—Biography.   2. Slick Boys (Rap group)—Biography.

3. Police social work—Illinois—Chicago.   4. Community policing—Illinois—Chicago.

5. Juvenile delinquency—United States—Prevention.   6. Violence—United States—Prevention.

7. Social action—United States.    I. Davis, Eric.

HV7911.A1S55    1998

362.70973—dc21                                                         98-16933

                                                                          CIP


ISBN 0-684-83300-X

# Acknowledgments

First of all we would like to thank some of the people who helped shape and form what is now the Slick Boys. Starting with our manager, Glenn Merrill (the unseen Slick Boy), and his family: Curba, Clarissa, Geraldine, Curba R., Nina, Marissa, Michael, Carol, and last but certainly not least, Adrienne. Our attorney, Steve Muslin, and his family (Steve, we can not begin to say how much you have always been there for us). Our crew, especially our dancers who have been so instrumental in our success. To Joel Goodman and Michael Merrill, the two people who helped make us "famous" because of the hard work and talent that they put into making our music videos. To Mr. Ernest Duarham, who helped to launch us in the beginning—Mr. D., thank you very much. To War-zone Records, Final Rise Productions, Party People Productions, and Smooth Sound Studios, the "sounds" behind the Slick Boys. To our homies, Jake and Dre—you really looked out for us. To Mary Ann Naples and Laurie Chittenden at Simon & Schuster, for believing in our message. To Seth Godin Productions, especially Lisa Di-Mona and Robin Dellabough—without you this book would not have been written. And to Luchina Fisher, who helped tell our story so brilliantly. Peace and much love.

—THE SLICK BOYS

# ACKNOWLEDGMENTS

To Carol, Alexandra, William Davis Sr., Adele Davis, Janice Davis, William Davis Jr., Kelly Davis, The Slumlords, Mr. and Mrs. Anton Kuzmanic, Gary Kuzmanic, Bob Kuzmanic, Ruth Kuzmanic, the Prenner family, the Franco family, the Terna family, the Triantifillo family, Jim Conlon, Velman Stevens, Don Russell, Guy Lewis, Swede Erickson, DeAndre, Gregory, Angela, Pooh, Marva, Tony, Tyreese, Mike Tolliver, Ron Yoshioka, Kevin Russell, Gary Morris, Lynden Rose and the Rose family, the Chicago Police Department, OFFICERS OF THE PUBLIC HOUSING SECTION (THE REAL POLICE), all of our friends from Cabrini-Green, Robert Taylor, Rockwell Gardens, ABLA Homes, Lathrop, and Ida B. Wells.

—ERIC

Praise to God, the foundation of my life. To the memory of Mrs. Estella McIntyre, who taught me how to believe in self. She taught me the true meaning of three basic, but important, values, which when used correctly could improve any community—"love, peace, and respect." She also taught me how to live my life and to help others. To my son Julian Kermit Martin, whom I live for. To my sisters and brothers Darlene, Glenn, Lashawne, Robert, Antawaun, Cedric, Drake, Julio, Deandre, Nikki, Regina, and Dee Dee. To Samuel and LuElla Finley and family, Richard and Mamie Bolden and family, Sam and Laureteen Bolden and family, John Bolden, Steve McIntyre, and the rest of my family and friends who were important in me becoming who I am today. To my extended family, the adults of Ida B. Wells, who really believed that the community was responsible for raising the children, especially the people on my block at 526 East 37th Place. To everyone living in public housing—believe in yourself and always strive to make a difference; life is what you make out of it. To everyone who supported the Slick Boys and to my crew and their families, Eric, Glenn, and Randy.

—JAMES

# ACKNOWLEDGMENTS

To my late parents, Mr. and Mrs. Monroe Holcomb, who molded and shaped their son into a caring and giving person. To all my brothers and sisters, family and friends, who put up with the last five years of not seeing a lot of me because of the mission that I feel I was given by the Lord. The mission is not over yet; the candle is still lit. Thank you. Special thanks to the two other members of the Slick Boys, James and Eric—it's been hard and fun but most of all we did it together. Another special thanks to all our crew members over the years, especially Elaine, whose dancing skills are second to none. Thanks to all the other dancers who have helped us over the years.

—FAHEEM

# Contents

CONTENTS

# The Slick Boys

# Places We're Making a Difference

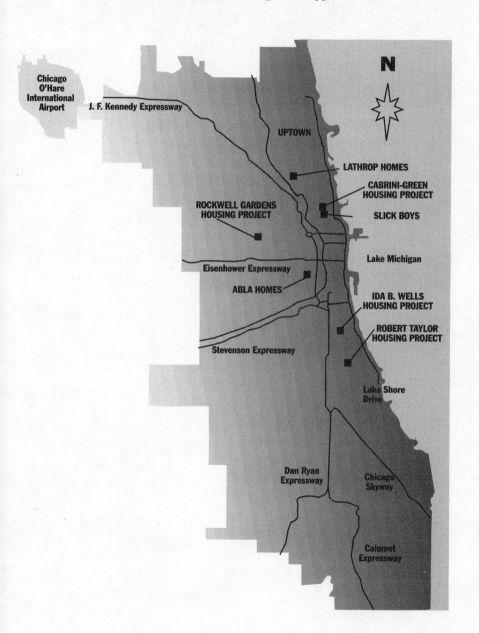

# One:

# What

# We've Done

# Introduction

*Dear Slick Boys,*
*Thank you for coming to Epworth. I really got some-*
*thing out of it, and I didn't even want to come at first,*
*knowing that y'all was the police. I didn't like the police*
*at first cause I was told they killed my father. But my*
*mother made me come anyway and I'm kind of glad*
*cause you showed me that all police ain't the same. I'm*
*grateful because I took my father's death out on all po-*
*lice, but you are okay.*
*    I did a lot wrong and I been through a lot on the*
*streets. I also see a lot, and since you be on the streets*
*and you see a lot, can you please answer a question for*
*me: When a child grows up in a messed up place and*
*ain't got no father and their mother's either on drugs or*
*just don't care, what do that child do to survive?*

RA RA, AGE 13

As plainclothes cops in Chicago's housing projects, we're faced
with that question every day. As children, we lived the life ourselves: I spent seven years in Cabrini-Green. James Martin grew up

in the Ida B. Wells project. Randy Holcomb lived across from the Rockwell Gardens project. We know what it feels like to be shot, to have a mother strung out on drugs, to go to sleep on the floor because of gunfire. But somehow we each did more than survive. We rose above our circumstances. We are well educated. One of us went to West Point. Another played in the NCAA Final Four basketball tournament. And the three of us have come full circle, back to our community to help other kids thrive. Not because we think we're better. The reason we came back to do the kind of work we do is that we have at least part of an answer to the question: "What does a child do to survive?"

Randy, James, and I are the Slick Boys. "Slick boys" is slang for undercover cops, which is what we are in our night job. Slick Boys is also the name of the rap music group we formed in 1990. During the day, we tour elementary schools and junior and senior high schools, rapping and telling our story to children for whom survival is a miracle. These students are caught up in a vicious cycle of drugs, gangs, and shattered families. When the Slick Boys arrive, they hear, maybe for the first time, that there is a different way. They see in us three living, breathing examples of a better life. They listen because we speak their language, and they listen because we listen back to them.

We took the opportunity to speak from our own experience because we were tired of seeing young brothers zipped up in body bags. "I was walking around Cabrini when it was buck-wild," James says. "They were shooting there every day like it was legal." With patience and perseverance, we have gained the trust and respect of Cabrini gang members: There have been no more gang wars at Cabrini-Green since we helped arrange a truce between rival gangs in 1992. How did we help to bring peace to this project? What do we do to help maintain it? Most important, what does this mean for the rest of the country?

Although we are from a place referred to as "the 'hood," we all live in neighborhoods: Not just a black teenager in Chicago, but a white housewife in Atlanta; not only a Vietnamese gang member in

Washington, D.C., but a Latino teacher in East Los Angeles. No matter where you live, we guarantee that within a few blocks there is a child who is hungry, a child who is abused, a child who is on drugs, a child at risk. We can't keep saying, "That's the government's job." It should be Americans helping Americans. Yet it seems to take a tragedy for us to reach out to one another. Because when something tragic happens, this country does round the wagons up. A building gets blown up in Oklahoma and we all pitch in. We can be wonderful once we get off our butts. Why should children have to die first?

Since we formed our rap group, the Slick Boys have been asked to perform for hundreds of school and community groups not only in Chicago, but in small towns, suburbs, and other urban areas across the country. We are able to reach more kids by taking what we have learned on the streets of Chicago to schools across the country. Some teachers and administrators who invite us to speak seem to expect miracles. They're hoping we'll be like a magic show and with a wave of our hands transform their children into smart, productive students. The truth is it takes more than magic. It takes cooperation, dedication, and hard work by parents, teachers, and students alike. The real miracle workers are the kids themselves.

Sometimes miracles do happen. In 1995, we were at University High School in Philadelphia. There must have been about 10,000 kids in the auditorium. After we performed, we encouraged students to ask questions or say what was on their minds. One boy, about sixteen, walked on stage and threw down his rag, which signified his membership in a gang. He was essentially saying "I quit."

"I can't die like this," he announced. "From this day on, if the opposition brings it or my boys bring it, I don't care. I got a family to take care of." As he walked to his seat, his boys parted to let him through.

That young man, who had just fathered a little baby, not only quit the gang but quit in front of his peers. He came to our program a boy and left a man. When a reporter asked me afterward if his life was now in danger, I told her, "If he dies, at least he'll die with honor and on his own terms."

It's rare that someone would quit a gang on the spot. But once kids hear what we have to say, many return to their communities and put down their rags and their flags and leave the gangs. That's one of our goals. We want kids to choose life—to make decisions that are truly in their best interest.

When we visit schools in the inner city, we feel like we're the big brothers, telling our younger siblings to "take our word on this." When we go to other schools, we travel in part as representatives of poor communities. We hope that we are teaching kids a thing or two about people they've never met and places they've never been to.

That's been the case wherever we've gone, including small towns and cities, where adults think their children won't relate to our message. Even after the school board invited us to perform in Dubuque, Iowa, some parents and teachers didn't think we needed to be there, in spite of several local drive-by shootings and subsequent deaths. I guess they hoped the violence would just go away. Or maybe they resented having three black men who work in the inner city talk to their white children about a gang problem. Thank goodness there were a few who recognized the seriousness of the situation.

While we were in Iowa, we saw two hundred to three hundred Black Gangster Disciples, and 75 percent of them were white. These weren't just wannabe gangsters. They were kicking butt and taking names. Gangs are not exclusively a "black" problem, or even an urban problem—they are everywhere in America today. In fact, in small towns and cities, as well as the suburbs and rural areas, gang members actually seem to gangbang harder. It's probably a lot easier for them to get a hold of weapons, since many of their parents keep guns at home for hunting. Especially in rural locales, kids have also been taught to shoot by their parents. Then, too, I suspect kids in smaller towns get into gangs simply because they're bored. And money also plays a part, particularly in the degree to which kids abuse controlled substances. They can afford keg parties, while inner-city youngsters are limited to passing around a couple of forty-ounce bottles of beer on the stoop.

But one of the main reasons kids get into trouble is the same whether they live in the suburbs or in the inner city: Children are seeking their parents' attention. Whether parents are simply too busy struggling to get by to give kids the attention they need, or too self-involved and preoccupied with doing their own thing, the end result is that their kids think they don't give a damn. Young people all over the country are experiencing similar problems. Our rap resonates with white kids in suburban schools just as much as it does with black kids in urban schools. Getting our rap to resonate with white suburban *parents* is a lot harder.

Haven Middle School in Evanston, Illinois, for example, is about 45 percent black and 55 percent white. There are significant economic differences within the community. When someone brought a gun into the building last year, it was a big deal. Nothing like that had ever happened at the school before. The principal called us, and we offered to attend a parents' meeting, where emotions obviously were going to run high.

When we first arrived, the parents were defensive. They felt that these incidents shouldn't be happening in a place like Evanston. We explained to them these problems are cropping up every place where kids have idle time and not enough parental supervision. We asked the parents to take a good look at themselves and their roles in their homes and community. If they felt they weren't doing enough, they should roll up their sleeves and do more. The gun at Haven Middle School was their wake-up call.

We wrote this book because we *all* need to be reminded that as individuals we can have an impact on other people's lives. Still, most of our battles are uphill. We save one person, another one dies. We send one to college, another goes to prison. We get one out of the gang, another falls prey to drugs. We try not to let it get us down. Even if we feel discouraged, we try to act upbeat and positive no matter what. Our attitude is that if we handle a situation incorrectly the first time, we're better prepared the next. Our belief in the great potential and basic decency of all human beings continues to inspire us and sustain our work. What we're trying to do is change lives, one life at a time.

We have a video out called *What You Gonna Do?*, which is about a number of social problems, from violence to homelessness to unemployment. We're saying, "What are we going to do as individuals? What are we going to do as communities to fix and eradicate these problems?" Too often, our apathy kills us. We wait for somebody—anybody—to come in and fix the problem. But no one comes to your house to clean your house. You have to clean your own house.

We're far from alone in our beliefs. People have been finding ways to help each other for years. We've run into kids as young as eleven and retirees as old as eighty tackling problems ranging from hunger, teen smoking, and pregnancy to drug abuse, gang violence, and homelessness. They're helping youth through sports, computers, travel, music, camping, dance, singing, and tutoring. There seems to be no end to the creativity of Americans when they set their mind to something.

Take 25-year-old Tonya LeNell Smothers, for example. When she moved to Birmingham, Alabama, her neighbors were isolated, held hostage by the fear of drug dealers and other crime. Tonya took it upon herself to develop a block watch. As captain, she encouraged her neighbors to open up, support one another, and take action. She organized outings for the neighborhood kids and held graffiti clean-up days.

Closer to our home is Joel Perez. Another former gang member, he wound up in Elgin, Illinois, a Chicago suburb where an estimated seven hundred gang members still are active. Joel tries to find gang members or kids at risk of joining and get them involved in his "God's Gym." Every day, he offers three hundred kids a place to go that's safe from street violence. They can play soccer, lift weights, receive tutoring, attend GED classes—and listen to Joel's streetwise wisdom.

Down in Seminole, Florida, David Levitt took his first step toward becoming part of a solution at the age of eleven. He was concerned about feeding the hungry and had noticed all the food that went unserved in his school cafeteria. Although several adults had tried to get the school to donate the leftover food, they had been told it would involve too much red tape. So David went directly to the county school board, who agreed to donate food from all ninety-two schools in the county. He then continued on this mission by enlisting restaurant owners and caterers to donate unserved food, getting manufacturers to donate containers for transporting food to shelters and soup kitchens, and taking food from a supermarket to a feeding agency. Now fourteen, he recently drafted and is lobbying for a resolution that's been introduced in the Florida state legislature. If passed, David's hunger-fighting methods will be duplicated all over the state.

Our philosophy is straightforward. It might be described as old-fashioned. We believe people should work hard and help themselves. If they follow this rule, people have more respect for themselves, their family, and their community. We don't think they should have to go it alone. We're really trying to *help* them help themselves. Our plan is based on ten principles. Some involve changing an attitude, or adopting a point of view. Others require more concrete action or work. These are the principles:

## 1. SERVE AND PROTECT YOUR BROTHERS AND SISTERS

Our version personalizes the official police motto, "To Serve and Protect," by reminding people that we are all related as human beings. It's at the heart of our belief that to be of use to others is the most important part of being alive. People think of police officers as those guys they see on TV in shoot-outs, kicking in doors, cars exploding. But the vast majority of the police work we do is more like social work or teaching. We want to be able to reach back and help our brothers and sisters behind us.

## 2. SPEAK THE LANGUAGE

We're not talking about speaking the language to only the kids in the 'hood. There is a language that we speak in America, a language that we haven't used to talk to one another in a long time. It's going into the neighborhood and learning about that particular neighborhood, so you're not just on the outside looking in, but on the inside looking out. It's the language of taking care of our whole community, giving positive strokes to all our kids. It's sitting down to talk with a younger person without talking above his head. That shows instantly that you're on the same wavelength, willing to listen.

### 3. BE A RAY OF HOPE

People turn toward hope as naturally as plants turn toward the sunlight. It's just a question of being there, shining that light of hope on them. It might take time, but by remaining optimistic and hopeful no matter how hard life seems to get, we believe you can turn around a life. You're a ray of hope when you say to a child, "Look, I've been through a lot of what you're going through. I made it because someone helped. Now let me help you."

### 4. DON'T PLAY TO THE STEREOTYPES

It would have been so easy for the three of us to stay the victims of the worst kind of stereotyping: black, poor, housing project equals drugs, dropouts, and death. We overcame these stereotypes and obvious plots and wrote our own life scripts. Today, as policemen, we try not to generalize about the young kids we encounter on the street. Think about it: How often have you made an assumption based on someone's skin color, clothing, speech, or taste in music? Or worse, based on what TV tells you, or what the news tells you, or what other people tell you? We're here to tell you: not all blacks sell drugs. All Hispanics don't gang bang. All whites are not in the Ku Klux Klan.

### 5. GIVE SOMETHING BACK

Unless we give back, there's no future. We're lost. We have to explain to our children how fortunate they are, instead of letting them believe they're entitled to money. Show them that you don't take anything for granted, that you're always going to give back to your community. Everyone's trying to be rich and famous, trying to get the bigger house, the bigger Mercedes. But before there were Mercedeses and mansions, there were human beings. Rich isn't having money; it's trying to make a difference in someone else's

life. If everyone in this country grew up and made even one con-
tribution to another person or group of people, imagine what a
wealthy country we would be.

## 6. EDUCATION IS KEY

You're a slave if you're not educated. Right now, we're spending
more money on penitentiaries than on schools. So if you're not educated, able to make choices, able to function in society, you're basically preparing yourself for a future in jail. School opens doors
that lead disadvantaged youth to productive adulthood. We've
never heard anyone say she was sorry she got a good education.
After all, we're put on this earth to develop our innate, God-given
capacities. We encourage every kid we meet to get the most education she can.

## 7. HAVE BIG EXPECTATIONS

Kids know when adults think they're doomed to failure. Too often it's a self-fulfilling prophecy. Expecting the best from kids often
means they'll reach and stretch and grow far beyond their own
wildest dreams. We tell them to dream extra large. Dream for the
stars and the moon and the whole galaxy. If you only have one
dream, and you fall short, then what? Never think low. If you're going to be a crook, lead other crooks. If you're going into the service, go in as an officer, not a private. If you want to go in the
kitchen, don't work in the kitchen: Own the kitchen. The higher
you aim, the higher you'll get.

## 8. RESPECT ONE ANOTHER

Respect is the first thing to go when a society deteriorates. Without respect, there can be no peace and there can be no progress.
With respect, anything is possible. We don't have to like each other
as individuals, but we have to respect one another's beliefs. This is
the foundation of a community, and it takes a whole community to
raise a child. If Johnny doesn't have respect for Mrs. Jones who lives

next door, maybe she'll look out the window, see Johnny doing something wrong, then turn her head. She's thinking, "He's a bad kid anyway." But if Johnny had been speaking to Mrs. Jones with respect whenever he saw her, then she would be more likely to intervene.

### 9. LEAD BY EXAMPLE

Kids soak up adults' behavior, whether adults realize it or not. By acting the way they want kids to behave, adults set the stage for kids to imitate them. If you drink a twelve-pack and sit in front of the TV when you come home every day, your child is learning that's how you're supposed to unwind. When it comes time for you to tell your child, "I don't want you drinking," he isn't going to hear that message. He's already been hearing you loud and clear for ten or fifteen years. Watch your own behavior before you try to tell anyone else what to do.

### 10. HELP PEOPLE ONE BY ONE, ONE TO ONE

We believe that's how to get things done—not by relying on government or committees or waiting for "society" to solve problems by helping the masses. We have to help individuals first. We've got to face the fact that some people don't want to be helped. So we have to help the next man who's reaching for the rope. Pull him up first. Then he can help others. It only takes one caring grandmother, teacher, dad, or cop to turn a troubled child around.

This book is organized around these ten simple principles. Each chapter turns on ways that both the Slick Boys and others have tried to use the principles. Cabrini may be an extreme example of a place to teach and learn these lessons, but, as our subtitle points out, we think these are life lessons that everyone can apply. As you're reading, think about how you might use each lesson in your own day-to-day life, be it in an inner-city neighborhood, college campus, suburban development, or small town.

This is our story as well as the story of countless others we've known in Chicago's projects and met as we've traveled around the country. It is an account of our three-man plan to forge a new relationship between police and community and to change the course of people's lives. We hope it will remind you of our humanity and oneness as a nation. As the Slick Boys, we offer a grassroots understanding of what's really happening on *all* our streets—and what we *all* can do about it.

# 1: Serve and Protect Your Brothers and Sisters

*When I die and people ask, "What kind of policeman was he?" I want them to say, "He made a difference in my life."*

—JAMES MARTIN

The "Village," on Chicago's West Side, was literally one of the city's darkest projects. There were no street lamps, and gang members had removed nearly all the lightbulbs in the building lobbies. It was summer of 1989 and a Friday night, too. With each tick of the clock, the place got a little warmer, the music a little louder, and the boys a little rowdier. By nine, the buildings were pitch-black but the sounds pouring out of the darkness signaled a party in progress.

The Village was a conglomeration of the Adams, Brooks, Loomis Court, and Abbot developments, also known as ABLA. It had a booming drug business, mostly because there were very few shootings. It was nothing to see fifteen or twenty dealers working a shift. That Friday night, they'd set up a card table just outside the building and people were lining up like customers at a fast-food restaurant.

Being a tactical officer in the Chicago Police Department's Public Housing unit meant responding to trouble wherever it broke out among the city's nineteen project developments. Randy's beat was Rockwell Gardens then, while James and I, partners since 1988, worked primarily in Cabrini-Green and ABLA. Another housing officer named Julius had accompanied me and Jimmy to ABLA that night to check out the situation.

Immediately, I spotted a man in a jacket running from the building. Wearing a jacket in summer is a dead giveaway that someone is packing something, usually drugs or a weapon. This guy was carrying both.

He was about 240 pounds, most of it muscle. The dude was bigger than me and taller than Jimmy. When we tried to handcuff him behind his back, he wrestled free and started to fight us.

Meanwhile, a mob of about fifty people had gathered outside. Julius was on crowd control and was getting jittery. Suddenly, some young dude jumped out of the crowd, pulled a gun from the dealer's discarded jacket, and ran inside the building. But we couldn't chase after him—we were still trying to handcuff the dealer. We had to subdue him before things turned ugly. Finally, we succeeded, but as we started walking him to the car, someone yelled, "Y'all ain't taking him nowhere."

"Call a 10-1 for officer assistance," I told Julius. "We got trouble."

My mind was racing. We got the guy raw. He's caught. So why were fifteen or twenty of his buddies circling us? This dude had to be the building's drug supplier. Then Jimmy and Julius dropped the prisoner, and we pulled out our guns and aimed them at the crowd. They responded by reaching under their jackets for their own weapons. "We're fucking y'all up," they shouted.

Now I had vowed to myself while I was at the Police Academy that no matter what, I was not going to die doing this job. I would use the common sense I got growing up on the streets to make the right decisions. I didn't want to have to shoot one of these fools. But just taking off was out of the question. There was no way we were going to turn ABLA over to these guys to sell drugs. We had something to prove, especially to the decent people who lived here.

"Step away," I told the mob. "We're the police. We're just doing our job." But nobody moved. These guys were juiced up, chanting "Fuck the police. Fuck the police."

We had to get their attention. Jimmy, who's got the biggest mouth of the three of us, shouted, "Hey, listen up! We're shooting women and babies first. We will not be the only ones dying out here."

Deep down, we were all pretty scared. But if those boys had known how scared we were, they would have killed us on the spot. The fact that we didn't act frightened made them hesitate. The women and children, who had been on the periphery of the mob, started backing away.

Suddenly, a squad car drove up the fire lane, scattering the crowd. Then we heard a loud *boom!* Somebody was shooting at us from the building.

In the confusion, Jimmy ran behind an abandoned Toyota Corolla, which had been left in the middle of the playground. Julius and I hit the ground. *Boom!* The dude had fired again. *Boom!* Julius screamed, "I'm hit, I'm hit," and his gun flew into the air. I went for it while Jimmy grabbed Julius and pulled him behind the car. When he shined his flashlight on Julius's head, he started to laugh. "Motherfucker, you ain't bleeding," I heard Jimmy say. "That's sweat." Julius had a huge knot on his forehead. Apparently, the bullet had struck the concrete, and a fragment had ricocheted and popped him on the head. Julius was going to be okay. At least for now.

I made another radio call: "Squad. 10-1. Emergency. We're pinned down. We're afraid the building behind us will start shooting." We knew that if that happened, we were fucked, because we would be in their crossfire. The dispatcher asked if we wanted the war wagon, the police mobile sniper unit. "Hell, yes," I said. "Send everything. They're shooting at us."

We figured the shooter had to be the same guy who'd snatched the drug dealer's gun, but we couldn't keep our heads up long enough to see anything except the muzzle flash when he fired. Those shots were coming every few minutes, and they sounded like they were being blasted from a cannon. Even so, we couldn't resist shining our flashlights at the building just to let him know we weren't dead yet.

The two white guys from the squad car scrambled next to us. Now there were five grown men trapped behind the little Toyota. "Cops can't carry Glocks," Jimmy said, looking at the type of gun they had in their hands. "Where do you guys work?"

"The University of Illinois," came the response.

"What the fuck you doing back here?" I asked.

"You called a 10-1," they said. "We came to help you."

Jimmy just shook his head. They were crazy, but we had to give them credit: At least they were here. We had seen only one Chicago police car pass by, and it was headed in the opposite direction.

After about thirty minutes, we figured no one else was going to show, so we decided to make a break for the fire station next to the shooter's building. "On the count of three," I said, "spread out and run your ass off." I couldn't even tell if the guy was still shooting— I was too busy running and praying I wouldn't get hit. Every one of us made it to the fire station uninjured. When my sergeant said we were lucky, I told him luck, hell—we were blessed by God.

Afterward, the commander on the scene led a team into the building and caught the sniper. He was a seventeen-year-old kid who worked for the dealer. Even though he had tried to take the lives of five officers, the judge gave him only two years for aggravated assault.

Julius got three days off for stress because he had been in a shooting just a month before. He transferred out of the unit later that summer. Jimmy and I were back at work the next day.

In fact, Jimmy and I worked ABLA every day for the next year. I think that intimidated the drug dealers more than anything else. They had to be thinking, "We threatened them—we shot at them— and those fools came back."

And we kept coming back. Whether it was ABLA, Cabrini-Green, or Rockwell Gardens, Jimmy, Randy, and I were always there. That was something new to the people in those neighborhoods. They weren't used to seeing guys who *wanted* to be there, who weren't saying, "I don't live here, so I don't care." When the decent folks saw that we were ready to help them *and* take on the bad guys, they started to believe that someone out there, that *cops,* truly cared about their community. The police motto, "To Serve and Protect," took on a whole new—and for the first time, *real*—meaning for them. They eagerly took us in, and started to make us a part of their community.

Not everybody was so hospitable, of course. We weren't as popular with the dope dealers and gangbangers, especially in Cabrini-Green. Cabrini itself was split among three gangs: the Vice Lords, the Gangster Disciples, and the Cobra Stones. The Disciples are by far the largest gang in Cabrini and in Chicago, numbering some 45,000 members. But the Cobras, the smallest gang in Cabrini, were the most vicious. If the Disciples shot at the Cobras one day, the Cobras shot back for at least two weeks. All of the Cobras were trained shooters, unlike the members of other gangs, some of whom only sold drugs or kept the books. The Cobras often joined with the Vice Lords to fight against the Disciples, who were trying to force both gangs out of Cabrini.

The Cabrini battle was about turf and the money to be made from selling drugs on that turf. But it was also about the older generation passing down its culture of violence to the younger generation. If you called yourself a Lord and another guy was a Disciple, that was enough to start a fight. You had guys shooting and killing one another over a bunch of dumb stuff, like wearing the wrong colors or messing with somebody's sister or because you were a Cobra. In Cabrini, violence had become a way of life.

A former leader of the Gangster Disciples, Vance "Vino" Simmons, now thirty-three, says Cabrini-Green was the roughest of the projects when he was coming up. He explains the territorial imperative felt by every gang member, saying, "Guys wanted their space, to establish some ground. Each gang, wherever they were living, wanted to be comfortable and not worry about the opposition sneaking up on them. You wanted to be able to say, 'This is my building,' even though you didn't own nothing."

While the Chicago Housing Authority owned the buildings in Cabrini, the gangs controlled them. They had essentially occupied them for their drug operations. Before 1992, the only security guards in the buildings were working for the gangs. Residents who had no part in the gangs were living in a concrete prison, forced to side with whichever gang controlled their building. The freedom to move about their neighborhood was severely limited. If you moved into 500 West Oak, you were going to be a Vice Lord, whether you liked it or not. Even old Miss Tiny, an elderly lady who sold sausages and snow cones out of her car, was shot while standing in front of 929 N. Hudson. Because she was on the Disciples' side of the projects, she was considered part of their team.

People like Miss Tiny made us want to work for the betterment of the entire community when we arrived in Cabrini. But first, we had to stop the gangs from shooting. And in order to do that, we had to prove that we were serious about making a difference on their own turf. We had to show them that we don't play, that we mean what we say, and that we're going to be back every day.

At first the gang members didn't show us much respect. For starters, they hadn't seen too many black plainclothes officers and certainly none as young as me and James. A lot of the guys we were arresting were older than we were. They'd see us and want to fight. "Man, I'll whip your young ass," they'd say. Or we would hear, "I ain't listening to you. The white police didn't tell us that." There's an attitude among black gang members that "can't no nigger tell me nothing." And since we are black, too, we went through many days of getting punched and punching back before the word finally got out: *If you come at them, they're going to stand their ground; they're not going to be run out of here.* In order to get a brother's attention, sometimes you have to go through his ass to reach his head. Once you've got the ass, the head can hear you loud and clear.

By playing the game their way, we both intimidated and impressed the gangs. But soon it was time for us to take our game to another level. We started by giving the gang members a list of rules to follow and we were consistent in enforcing them. For example, we'd tell them, "If you're back selling dope on this corner tomorrow, we're going to lock you up." They would respond, "Well, you might as well mark it on your calendar, nigger, because we'll be back here tomorrow." That's just how they talked to the police. But we were back on that same corner the next day, ready to make some arrests. The gangs quickly learned that our word was our bond.

Those first couple of years, we were making about four hundred arrests annually. Sometimes we had as many as seven prisoners in the back of our car. It wasn't unusual to see us marching a line of bangers in handcuffs across the blacktop. But then some of the gang members started threatening *us* with prison. They charged us with police brutality and accused us of stealing money, trading guns, and even of robbing and killing people. Of course, none of these accusations were true. What *was* true was that we were hurting business in Cabrini and the gang members figured if they couldn't bury us, maybe the police department would. So they started filing false beefs against us. At one point, Jimmy and I had as many as twenty-eight complaints pending. None of the charges, all of which Internal Affairs checked out, were substantiated. But this experience *did* change the way we did police work. For all the locking up we were doing, the shooting still hadn't stopped. So we quit chasing the big crooks—the wheelers and the dealers—and started talking to the kids.

By then we had managed to get the gang members' attention. Some listened to us out of fear, others out of respect. Talking to them was not a problem since we spoke the same language. We understood where a lot of these brothers were coming from. I had been in a gang growing up and both Randy and James had brothers who were in gangs. We had all experienced poverty up close and knew how it felt to be on the outside of society.

Once we had their attention, we poured as many positives into their heads as we possibly could. The first thing we told them was, "You are men. You are *not* Nigger Machine Gun Kelley. You're *not* Boo Man. You're *not* Dog. You're *not* Gangsta. When you call yourselves those things, you become them." In a sense, we were training them to be men. We told them what it means to be a brother, a father, a member of their community; we told them that to be a man means to assume responsibility for your actions. We told them we were going to hold them accountable for being responsible—for making sure the shorties went to school, for instance.

We knew how important order was in the lives of the bangers, and consistency. But we were learning the necessity of communication too, of speaking to these men in their own language. The older guys started sharing with us their anger, their frustration at the police. They talked about what they wanted for their kids, their little brothers and sisters. Without fail, they wanted their children to have a better life than they had. As corny as it sounds, they wanted them to share in the American dream. Speaking the language of young people essentially means listening to them—not judging them as you offer support and guidance. For many of these youngsters, we became father figures. To their parents, we were their "lookouts," as one mother called us: "You were my eyes where my eyes couldn't go." Sometimes we were successful, sometimes we weren't. But we always tried.

I can't tell you how many times they threatened to kill me and Jimmy. Guys would tell us, "There's a hit out on y'all." When we asked who, they'd say, "The Whites," meaning the white buildings in Cabrini. So we started policing the Whites more, just to show them we weren't intimidated.

Jimmy had a simple philosophy: If I can die, then you can die. This meant that he was not going to let threats stop him from policing these projects. We all feel that way. It's crucial that the good people know they've got somebody who can—and will—stand up for them. Because if the troublemakers can intimidate us, and we're the last defense between the good citizens and them, then we're all truly lost. And if you live for nothing, then you'll die for nothing. So when we came to Cabrini, we made up our minds that the people here were going to get police service, whether they liked it or not.

That's how it got started for Randy, Jimmy, and me. By coming back every day and risking our lives, we got these larger-than-life reputations in the community. We were infamous long before we were famous. We were *slick boys,* which is slang for undercover cops, before we became the *Slick Boys.*

Once Jimmy and I got into a shooting in front of building 660 in Cabrini. According to the neighborhood folks, our bulletproof vests were all shot up, yet we still kept firing our guns. That got people saying, "They can't be killed." But as Jimmy points out, if we did half the things folks said we did, we'd either be dead or superhuman.

The community gave us our own street names, a sort of honor. In the projects, just about everyone has a name they use on the street: Rat, Insane Wayne, Scotty G., Dirt. . . . Some people we know only by their street names. And some people know us only by ours. I became 21 because I play basketball and 21 is game point. James was nicknamed Eddie Murphy, because he was always signifying on people—in other words, he would arrest a guy, then joke with him and talk about his mama. Randy's nickname is Faheem, which in Arabic means "understanding one." Of the three of us, he's the nicest. He would sooner talk to you than lock you up.

Our reputations were just as notorious as any gangster's. When we'd step into projects on the South Side, such as Robert Taylor or Altgeld Gardens, and identify ourselves as police, guys would say, "Oh, 21, Eddie Murphy, Faheem, what y'all up to?" People would even take pride in being arrested by us. To get locked up by a bluecoat—a uniformed cop—was an embarrassment. But if Jimmy or I arrested you, it meant you were real bad. Guys could ride on telling their buddies that 21 and Eddie Murphy got them. They knew that if Randy arrested them, he was really trying to tell them to get their act together. People were looking for somebody to believe in, to trust. They wanted a hero, even if it was an antihero. And we became both.

Folks seemed to relate to us. For instance, we might be the eighth police car to arrive at a shooting. Other officers would be trying to figure out what had happened, saying they didn't have the story yet. But then we'd hear, "Hey, Faheem, Eddie Murphy, 21, see that guy standing over there in the blue shirt? He did the shooting and the gun's under the car." People would wait for us to arrive. Or they would see something and hit us on our pagers. When we'd say, "We're not working," they'd answer, "I'll tell y'all tomorrow, then. I ain't telling them other police. I don't know them." We'd take time off and when we came back, the old ladies would tell us, "Y'all can't take no vacations that long anymore." It was like we were becoming the community's own private police force.

Reputation is everything in neighborhoods like the ones where we work. Reputation is what makes the good folks trust you and the bad ones fear you. It can actually save your life. If the bad guys think you're fearless—if they think you're not scared of them, that you're not scared of dying—they'll think twice before trying something.

Our reputation did more police work than anything else in Cabrini-Green. The gangbangers had been shooting almost daily there for ten years. But as hard as a lot of them thought that Jimmy and I were, they eventually realized we were also fair. They knew that we didn't take the battles between them and us personally, that we understood they were living in a violent world and were used to dealing with each other violently. When they did right, we treated them just like anybody else. They also knew that if they really needed something, they could come to us. If we felt they had been wrongly accused of a crime, we would even testify on their behalf. We acted as a buffer between them and other police. And we helped bring them to the table so they could finally lay down their guns and their differences and make peace with one another.

# 2: Speak
# the Language

*Start off*
*at the age of five;*
*you was cockin' your hat*
*cause you thought you were live.*
—FROM "AIN'T IT A SHAME" BY THE SLICK BOYS

In order to be peace officers as well as police officers in the projects, Randy, Jimmy, and I had to establish peace among Cabrini-Green's gangs. That meant we had to reach out to the kids, who become bangers as young as ten years old. The lure of the gangs is simple. They give kids everything society denies them: money, status and respect, and perhaps most important of all, a sense of family. The stories of young lives wasted, ruined, and destroyed by gang life are too numerous to fit within the pages of any one book. But one story stands out as a symbol for the rest.

We used to walk the building at 500 W. Oak all the time. Most of the calls were for Anette Freeman, whose neighbors kept complaining that she was leaving her young son, Dantrell, at home alone. First, we'd go over to Wells Street, where we knew the boy's father hung out, always up to no good. We'd find him and he'd say,

"She's the woman; she needs to be watching him." Then we'd go searching for her, which was never easy because she had a fierce drug problem and was always out hustling to feed her habit. When we'd catch up with her, we'd remind her that if she kept leaving her son by himself, he was going to get hurt.

One day, we got a report of a fire at her apartment. When we arrived, the door was locked. Anette had always told her son, "Lock the door and don't let anyone in while Mommy's gone." We could hear the little boy in there screaming but he wouldn't come to the door. Finally, we kicked it in. There he was, his face and hands burned. The couch where he had been sitting was engulfed in flames. We learned later that he had been playing with matches. That was in the spring of 1992.

In the fall of 1992, just after Dantrell turned seven, he and his mama were walking to school when a sniper's bullet rang out. Dantrell was killed while holding his mother's hand. That shot silenced all others and forced the leaders of the three gangs in Cabrini to call a cease fire. Not that they had much choice. The block was hot, as they say. With all the police, politicians, and reporters flooding the area, they had to keep a low profile until the heat was off. After all, gang leaders consider themselves businessmen, too, and while no one had paid much attention to their business during the ten-year war, now everyone seemed to be interested—including us. We saw an opportunity to get the gang members to put their guns down for good. So did former resident Marian Nzinga Stamps. Known as "Mama of Cabrini" because of her community activism, Marian had arbitrated nearly every squabble that had gone down in the projects. She was instrumental in finally bringing the gang leaders to the peace table by forcing the brothers to acknowledge their role in the death of neighborhood children. She shamed them with her words, saying, "We're killing our babies now? Not even animals do that."

If Marian was the mouthpiece, then we were the muscle. We told the fellas that if they didn't help put a truce together, they would have *us* to answer to. We vowed to give them up to the other police officers in the area. We knew their real names and where they lived, so this was no idle threat. The bangers realized that once their identities were exposed, the police would be on them every chance they got. They had no alternative but to cooperate: The leaders agreed to sit down.

Between fifteen and twenty young men representing the Cabrini gangs—the Vice Lords, Cobras, and Gangster Disciples—gathered at Marian's community organization, Tranquillity Marksman, to hammer out the terms of a truce. They were all tired of the violence but they didn't trust each other, so no one said much at first. Marian finally opened up the discussion by remembering all the kids who had been killed and how unsafe it was to walk across the blacktop, go to school or to the supermarket, or play in the park. That started the gang members talking about the dozens of young men they'd lost and the pain they'd lived with. "We've all lost someone," Wallace "Gator" Bradley, the Disciples' spokesman, said. "But what we're trying to do now is stop the body count. That's where everybody has to bring their minds to."

Once everyone agreed on the principle of peace in Cabrini, the discussion shifted to strategies for enforcing it. It was agreed that whoever violated the truce would be punished by members of their own gang. Such punishment would most probably be a beat-down, but we felt it was important for them to decide on such issues themselves. By giving the gang members responsibility for their situation, we were again saying, "We respect you as men and we expect you to *be* men." The gang members are vital members of the community. They are the fathers, sons, and brothers of the neighborhood. It's important that they make the decisions for the well-being of their community, if those decisions are going to stick. It was agreed that if one gang decided to break the truce, then the other two, along with the slick boys, would join together to knock them back into line. That was never a problem, though, because all three gangs decided peace was in their own best interests. After ten years of fighting and killing, a truce was declared in Cabrini.

On that day, over four hundred gang members stood outside the buildings. Each gang still huddled together, uncertain as to whether the truce was for real. We stood at the ready, too, as our commander had requested, to make sure other police officers would not misinterpret the presence of so many young men as the start of another fight. After eyeing each other for several minutes, some of the brothers from the different gangs started talking to each other. Then, they started shaking each others' hands and hugging. A lot of them had grown up together and actually liked one another. Some had even been best friends in grammar school but had ended their friendships when they joined opposite gangs, which was determined solely by what building they lived in. Seeing them get reacquainted was a magical moment we'll never forget. It was a day they thought they'd never see, but we'd known it was coming.

But I couldn't help thinking, "It's too late for Dantrell." We always said that he was destined for an early death. Dantrell lived a tough life, too tough for any child, but not unlike that of so many others in the projects. Had he lived a few more years, he probably would have been one of those boys selling crack or shooting into a crowd of kids.

The real cause of Dantrell's death was the absence of love and respect in his home and his community. Dantrell's mother, who gave birth to him at age fourteen, was too preoccupied with her addiction to take care of him. By the time his relatives and neighbors cared enough, it was too late for Dantrell, just as it is for so many. Dantrell Davis lost his chance when he was only seven years old—the victim of gang warfare. But Dantrell did not die in vain. His tragic death forced the truce that has allowed others their own precious chance.

The spirit of peace spread throughout the city. By the spring of 1993, all of Chicago's gang leaders had agreed on a citywide truce. Because some of the same leaders have out-of-state ties, Minnesota and Milwaukee gangs also put down their guns. The truce held up most of the summer before some of the gangs started fighting again; but, in Cabrini, peace is still pretty much the rule. For months after the gangs first signed the treaty, their leaders would meet once a week to talk out any beefs. After that, any time trouble flared up, they would quickly assemble and quash it. They proved that they could take care of their own problems, even after we left. Once everyone in Cabrini—the gang members as well as the residents—got a taste of peace, there was no way they were to going to let it slip away.

A couple weeks prior to the 1996 Democratic Convention in Chicago, there were six shootings, including one death, in Cabrini, after a senseless argument between a young woman and a young man turned into a gang fight. Local politicians and reporters were predicting that the truce was over. We were out of town at the time, but our pagers were buzzing constantly. It seemed that everyone in Cabrini was trying to reach us. As soon as we returned to Chicago, we headed over to the Green. After locating Boo and Dirt, two leaders of the Disciples, we said, "Hey, can y'all do us a favor?" They knew we wanted them to stop the violence. And they did. They agreed to rein their guys in, as well as to pay the funeral expenses of the young man who had been killed. That part of the conversation lasted all of thirty seconds. The rest of the time we hung out together, cracking jokes and talking about the old days. We had been chasing Boo and Dirt since they were little boys. We knew them and they knew us. We had a relationship—one built on mutual respect. Out of that respect came trust, the quintessential ingredient in any human accord, especially peace.

The way to gain the trust that is key to establishing a relationship with these kids is to speak their language. That's the only way they will even begin to hear you. We know the value of communication. Without it, the Cabrini peace would have never held—or even been established. We will speak to anyone in these communities in an effort to change lives and make them better. That includes gang members and their leaders, who, in the chaos of the inner city, often provide the only semblance of leadership and stability the community has. Given this tragic truth, it is better for both the community and the police if a gang is organized and has a strong leader. Then you can go to the head instead of the feet. It's easier to make the gang more accountable for its role in the community and eventually change that role by showing them more constructive ways to use their organization. Most gang leaders actually keep order among the bangers. Goody, one of the street leaders of the Gangster Disciples, is a prime example. He tells youngsters to stay in school, to stop dealing dope, to respect women. Goody is hardly a perfect role model, but the reality is that gangs do exist—in ABLA homes and Cabrini-Green, in inner city and, yes, in suburban neighborhoods throughout the country. And as long as they exist, they must be recognized, reckoned with, and, when possible, worked with. That's our philosophy, and dealing with the gangs directly has made for more success than not.

Ironically, this strategy is regarded with suspicion and mistrust by some. Our own motives for working with the gangs have even been called into question. We found that as our success—and our relationship—with gang members in Chicago's ghettos grew, some police officers started to malign our association with them. We have been accused of being gang members ourselves and were even investigated by the department. Once, a sting was set up to net some dirty cops selling drugs. After the sting went down, some cops in that division called to say that officers had expected to bust *us,* and had even warned other police that one of us was an ex-banger, another a Vice Lord, and that we were all known shooters! This just goes to show that you have to be true to what you believe in, no matter what. At the end of the day, all you'll have is your own dedication and conviction.

Randy, who grew up on the West Side, knows a lot of the boys, including Terry Young, a former leader of the Vice Lords. His brother and Randy were good friends growing up. "After I started working in Rockwell," Randy explains, "Terry and I were outside talking one day. His buddies saw him and started saying that he and I were cousins. Then it became brothers, then fellow gang members. Eventually, community people as well as the police were saying that I was a leader of the Vice Lords. That put Internal Affairs on my back but it didn't stop me from talking to people. Through my relationship with Terry, I was able to get a lot of fights squashed. I was like a tightrope walker, balancing on this thin wire all day long. Everybody was trying to push me over to their side."

One thing is certain: Regardless of the risks to us from both sides, we'll keep talking. The only way things can change is if both sides communicate. Cops and gang members have to learn to speak the same language—by listening to one another.

Once there was relative order among the gangs in Rockwell and Cabrini, we could reach out to others, especially the children, and focus on the "service" part of our job. "When we started talking to kids and telling them, 'Y'all don't need to be with all that gang stuff,' they looked at us and said, 'Okay, if y'all say so,' " Randy relates. "They took our word because they knew we had been through hell with them, with their fathers, their older brothers."

At this point, we realized we needed to tone down our own "bad" reputation in the community. Too many good people were as afraid of us as they were the Gangster Disciples. Forming the Slick Boys helped because it gave us a hook for communicating on another level. Once we became the Slick Boys, our service role became clear. Some of the guys we'd locked up even wrote us from prison, asking us to look out for their children.

Police actually *serving* these communities was a new concept. Previously, police hadn't even wanted to be there—officers weren't exactly volunteering to work in the projects. To be frank, most officers were sent to Public Housing because they'd messed up somewhere else. Housing was a dead end—and you could very easily end up dead. The same year we got into the standoff at ABLA, Jimmy and I were in three more shootings. We could have been in a shooting every day at Cabrini; violence was that common there.

Housing North was so full of misfits that we called the unit "F-Troop," a reference to the old TV comedy about cavalry fuck-ups. We were actually proud to be F-Troop—we even had F-Troop hats made—because the truth was, we worked our butts off. Only forty officers in Housing North handled a total of seven projects. Clearly, as such a small unit, we had to be one of the most active.

Policing strategy has improved significantly, as has the rapport between the cops and the community. It's very gratifying to see where and how we've made a difference. The key to this success is remembering that the police are, or should be, public servants. We couldn't just keep locking people up, because we realized it was getting us and the community nowhere.

Cops all over this country are taught to be police officers but not necessarily *peace* officers. The police academy only deals in right and wrong. The formula is "You do something wrong, we lock you up." So what Randy, James, and I decided to do—because we kept seeing the violence, we kept seeing the death—was to go one step further and try to *understand*. We wanted to understand why a brother would shoot an A-K into a crowd of boys he sits in class with during the day. How can he shoot guys he knows, whose funerals his mama is going to attend? Because they live across the street? Because they're wearing red and he's wearing blue? What's it really about? When we started asking those questions, we opened first one door, then another, and then another. And you don't need to be a cop to make a difference—anyone can try to understand.

What we see most days is very depressing. To hear a kid from the projects say, "They're talking about how I'm going to get killed out here, but I'm dead already. I was dead when I was born" . . . that knocks you back a step. You say to yourself, *Man, he's living with no dreams*. Then you think, *Is it really safe for me to work with people who don't think they have a way out?*

You have to be a strong person to make up your mind to get the best you can out of this situation. It's easier to write off the people who live in the projects, and that's what most cops do. They think, *They're going to end up in jail anyway*. That makes it easier for them to go through these projects like robots, with no feelings and no purpose.

But when you choose to come to the projects as a human being, you have to go to another level. Your work—your commitment—doesn't just stop after eight hours. Believe me, it's easier to make two arrests and forget about it. Then it's over. When we go home, we keep thinking about our people: "I've got to get that girl in the GED program"; "This boy is sixteen and got a girl pregnant, he's looking for a job"; "That kid is being hunted down, so I got to go talk to the rival gang and see if I can get the hit taken off him."

We're not the only police officers who've tried to truly serve those we protect. For example, the C.O.P. program is a division of the Pittsburgh Police Department. It stands for Community Oriented Police and maintains a force of over one hundred police officers, who work to establish a positive relationship and rapport with the neighborhoods to which they're assigned. Through ministations and community-oriented involvement, these cops reach right out to those most at risk. One young girl was a gang member at age fifteen when a C.O.P. officer befriended her and recommended her for a special Girl Scout troop based in her school. This girl wound up dropping out of the gang and working in the Girl Scouts' local office, and is now attending college through scholarship funds raised by C.O.P. and the Girl Scouts.

When we get out of our police cars these days, we have to be Everyman. Yeah, we're the guys who lock you up when you do something wrong, but we're also your friends. Your fathers. Your teachers. Your social workers. Your preachers. Your brothers. We have to wear many hats if we're going to be good police officers and good human beings.

We never forget that we're cops, but we also try to be people— people from the same place as those we're policing. In the following chapters, the three of us describe where we came from.

# Two:

# Where We

# Come From

# 3: Have

# Big Expectations

*My parents moved our family out of Cabrini-Green as*
*soon as they were able. But as an adult, I returned to*
*the projects as soon as I was able. This is the story of*
*how I completed that circle, of how I came "home," not*
*only to my community, but to myself.*

—ERIC DAVIS

I have "made it" by our society's standards. I escaped the gangs,
went on to college, and even played in the NCAA Final Four basketball tournament. But that success did not come easily. I had to
be shocked into turning my life around. I was only able to make
the right choices because I had a loving, stable family supporting
me, along with teachers and coaches who truly cared.

We started off in Cabrini. My parents had come from South Carolina with my sister Janice to the Great Lakes Naval Base in
Chicago, where my dad was stationed. Not long after that, they
moved into Cabrini-Green.

Once my dad got out of the service, my parents had planned to
go back to South Carolina, where all our relatives live. But they
kept having kids instead. My brother William, whom we call Man,

was born in 1955. Five years later, in May 1960, I came along. My brother Kelly was born two years after me. Dad found a job as a chauffeur for Robert H. Anderson, the national vice president of Sears Roebuck, and we made Chicago our home.

Cabrini then was nothing like Cabrini now. There were grass lawns and fines for walking on them. Residents kept the hallways and balconies clean, so children had a place to play. Older men called boys "young brother" and rapped about education and representing the community. Everyone I passed on the street on report card day wanted to know how I had done. Most of all, just about everyone there was working toward something better. Folks weren't planning on staying in the projects.

After 1967, things started to heat up in Chicago. The city erupted in violence—race riots, Vietnam War protests, and the 1968 Democratic National Convention street brawl. In Cabrini, we saw members of the Black Panthers and the Black Stone Rangers on a daily basis. I used to play with their little brothers. But my parents, especially my mom, didn't like these influences on us. Mom pushed for us to move, and both she and my dad worked two jobs to save enough for us to get out of Cabrini.

When I was seven, we moved to an apartment in Uptown. What my mom liked most about Uptown was that it was an integrated neighborhood with an integrated school. That was a big deal back then, and the school was full of students from all kinds of places. Besides the Appalachian kids, there were Vietnamese kids, Hispanic kids, even African kids. I learned early on that I wasn't inferior to anybody. I saw white boys, Asian boys, and brothers, and some were dumber than me and some were smarter. It had nothing to do with where they were from or the color of their skin.

I could also travel the world through my friends. At one buddy's house, I'd take off my shoes and listen to him converse with his parents in Vietnamese. I could hear—and eat—Italian at another friend's. They would both come over to my house and eat collard greens and fried chicken and say, "Man, I love this."

Sadly, some of my old friends from the neighborhood won't even tell people they're from Uptown. I guess they've bought into the American ideal of suburbs and segregation. The irony is that if

I told people I was from some Chicago suburb like Northbrook or Highland Park, they wouldn't want to believe me. They want to hear that I grew up on a dirt farm down South or in the projects. I believe my old friends and I have an obligation to say we're from Uptown, to tell people, "It isn't like you think. I know because I was there." Once people heard how cool it was to live in a mixed community, they might say, "I want my kid to have that experience, too."

I'm sure one of the reasons we all got along so well was because everybody was poor. About the only English the Vietnamese and Italian boys' parents knew was "food stamps." My family received government assistance and food stamps off and on. And none of us kids, whether we were black, white, or Asian, wanted to go to the grocery store to spend those food stamps. We used to have a saying: "I tote 'em, you sport 'em." The one who "sports 'em" had to hand the food stamps to the clerk. I always made my brothers pay for the groceries, and I "toted 'em." To me, carrying those food stamps was the ultimate in shame. Those were some big stamps.

Like others in the community, my parents were always working, trying to earn a dollar and provide for our future. I respected them for that, but I hated seeing what they went through. My mother worked for an old-fashioned steam dry cleaner. Her hair was always drenched when she came home from work. She used to get her hair done on Saturday, go to work looking nice on Monday, and return that night like she had worked in the fields all day.

It especially made me angry to see my father opening car doors. He was quiet but real sharp. When I was twelve, I told him, "You know, Dad, I hate that you have that job. I hate that you have to do that kind of shit."

His answer surprised me. "I hate it too."

"Why you doing it then?" I asked him.

"Sometimes you don't do what you want to do. You do what you *gotta* do. And if this is what puts food on my family's table, then this is what I will do."

From that day, I knew my daddy was a real man.

Finally my parents saved up enough money to buy a couple of bars, one on Leland and another on Wilson. Cops would come in, put on a sweater or jacket, and sip their drinks at the bar. Naturally, they drank for free. My parents never knew when they might need something from them. Prostitutes also worked the bar, but they were different then. They weren't like drug prostitutes today, always looking for a quick high. These women were strictly in the business of prostitution. Then there were the hustlers who made their money at the pool tables.

My parents had their own little hustle too. Back then, the bars ran a lot of the gambling, especially crap shooting and roulette wheels. Folks would come straight from the El stop on Broadway, cross the street to the bar, and get their gambling on. But my mom and dad had to know you or they wouldn't let you gamble.

We never thought of gambling as a crime because the way my parents ran it, nobody ever got hurt. I remember one man who lost all his money gambling. His wife came into the bar the next day and explained that he had gambled away their rent money. My dad peeled off $600 from a wad of bills and just handed it over to her.

People also came to my dad when they needed a loan. In those days, black folks couldn't go to some white bank for a loan. Getting the money from a family member or a hustler was the only way.

Eventually, Mom quit the cleaners and worked the bar business full-time. Dad kept his chauffeur job during the day and worked the bar at night. They did what they had to do, which meant raising each of us to be strong and independent so that we could take care of ourselves. My parents—and most others these days—couldn't be there all the time. They were too busy trying to make a better life for us.

I started hanging out at the playground behind McPherson Grade School when I was eleven. I said I went there to shoot hoops, but I was really checking out the older guys, the fellas from the Vice Lords, the Gaylords, and the Maniac Drifters. Talk about independent. They had money in their pockets and girls all around them. I wanted to be just like them.

"We're going to save you a corner, shorty," one of them would say. They'd polish off a beer, then hand me the bottle. There was only foam left but I still felt like I was drinking beer with the big boys. Sometimes they would send me over to the liquor store. Just knowing that nobody dared mess with me because I was on an errand for the gang was enough to give me juice.

Soon I was friends with a lot of the gang members, and some even became like my big brothers. My own older brother, William, and I didn't have a real good relationship. In fact, we hated each other. He used to bully me all the time, and when someone else pushed me around, he never stepped up for me. I knew the guys in the gang would always have my back. So when one of them asked me if I wanted to join the gang, I didn't hesitate.

The initiation ceremony was held at night. One guy went through all the rules, another said some prayers. Then one of the leaders held out his hand like a Mafia don for me to kiss his ring. After that, all the other members kissed and hugged me. At age twelve, I was in. It's sad how something that starts out so lovingly can end up so violently.

At that time I was living on Ainsle Street near Ashland Avenue. My parents had saved up enough money to buy a house in an all-white neighborhood a little farther west in Ravenswood. We were the first black family in the neighborhood, and racism was a whole new thing for me. That people would hate me just for the color of my skin had never occurred to me. But my little brother Kelly and I learned pretty quickly that when they call you "nigger," you can only let it run down your back for so long. Soon I was fighting damn near every week at school. I had decided that any time someone called me or my little brother "nigger," we were going to fight. Either people were going to get tired of calling us nigger, or we were going to get tired of fighting.

Being a part of the gang made it easier to go to school. It was like having an insurance policy. If guys stepped to me, they were also going to have to step to my boys. There were fifteen of us in the set: eight brothers, three Puerto Rican boys, and four white guys. In neighborhoods such as Uptown and Humboldt Park, it was common to have multiracial gangs because of the different ethnic groups in the area.

I hung out with a cat named Red Dog, a white boy with long red hair. He was a Maniac Drifter, twenty-three years old and just back from the 'Nam. Red Dog used to say, "I ain't never been to the County. I ain't never been to the penitentiary. I ain't never been to the district lockup." I immediately decided this is who I wanted to be like. He was making money. He had all these sisters and Puerto Rican girls crying over him. He used to give long head sessions, where he'd just spit out knowledge that was real. I still use some of those lessons today.

"Man, look, you got to understand you're in business, the business of being criminal," he'd say. "The first thing you have to understand is who the teams are. Police are on one team. You're on the other team. You got the friendly cops in the neighborhood, you got the hard-core cops, you got the cops you want to strangle. Every neighborhood has them all. The friendly cops come and everybody runs up to the car. 'Hey, what's up, Joe'; 'Hey, Bob.' And all the time you're around there, people are calling you by your nickname. 'Hey, Spanky.' 'Hey, Money-Money.' The cop sees you and ties your face to your nickname. A month later, Spanky shoots at Joe two blocks away. The cop knows who Spanky is and where to find him.

"So when the cops come up, you cut out. They stop me, I say, 'Yes, sir?' 'What's your name?' 'Ric.' 'You got an ID?' 'No.' 'Where you live?' 'Cross the street. I'm heading there right now, officer.' Short, direct, be on your way. Don't let them know you, because *you* don't want to know *them*. When you get to know each other, the game is up."

And that's how it would it be. We would sit in McPherson playground, and he would just kick it. I remember one night, Red Dog decided to fix me up with a woman.

Red Dog and me, and this brother named Wayne Bone, got in Wayne's blue Firebird and headed down Lawrence Avenue to Broadway, where the hookers hung out. This little white girl came up to the car, and she and Red Dog started talking. "You've got to give me some money if I'm goin' to go out with him," she said.

"Baby, we got the money," said Red Dog, handing her a $50 bill.

The girl put the money in her purse and said, "Let's go over to my place. We'll take care of the business. Then I can come back out here and do what I gotta do and y'all can move on."

But as soon as we got in the house, Red Dog started taking off his clothes. "Y'all look around," he said. "I'm goin' to get with her."

I stayed in another bedroom waiting my turn. As I looked around, I thought this had to be the pimp's main lady. She had a waterbed, and a nice stereo and TV. Then I opened the closet and saw racks of men's suits, hats, and shoes. This was the pimp's crib!

I stripped off my clothes and tried on a white suit. Then I put on a big white hat with a blue feather in the brim. "Man, I'm up," I said, laughing as I stared at my reflection in the mirror. "I'm keeping this suit, too."

Bone came into the bedroom with a bag full of stuff he'd stolen from the living room. Now I really wanted to get out of there. Meanwhile, Red Dog was tying the girl up with her underwear. "Hey, whatchu doing to her?" I asked.

"We just need to get out of here," he said. "Don't you say nothin' either."

Bone and Red Dog packed up all the stuff in the car. I had spied a nice Schwinn ten-speed, so I decided to ride that home. All of us were dressed like pimps, with open silk Mack shirts and big stack shoes on. I must have looked like a fool, riding a ten-speed dressed like a pimp. But no one could have told me that—except maybe my moms.

Two days later, the prostitute came looking for us. She wanted to know if she could work for us. Apparently, when her pimp came home and found all his stuff missing, he beat her and threw her out. I guess she figured we were the only ones who could protect her.

Young women often become prostitutes because they are looking to be cared for. The sad truth is they are just prey. For us they were a quick and ready source of cash. One way the gang made money was by shaking down hookers. Every night, they would line up on Broadway and each would pay us $10. If their pimps tried to stop us, we beat them up. We'd clear $300 or $400 a night. That was a lot of money back then, so much that none of us could take it home. We had to put it in a coffee can and dig up a corner of the playground sandbox and hide it there. We were so tough we couldn't even bring the money home. Ain't that crazy?

Personally, I preferred making money to gangbanging. I didn't like all that knocking out and getting knocked out. Besides, I thought I was smarter. I knew that there was more money to be made out there.

But I did have to fight at least once a week for the gang. And I also lost some of my friends.

The death that stands out the most is the first one I experienced. I was in fifth grade, not quite a banger yet, when the teacher announced that my homey Shelton Little had died. Everyone knew that Shelton used to sniff glue and aerosols. One day he was honking spray Pam and had a heart attack. For the rest of the school year, I sat next to his empty desk. It's an image that stays with me to this day.

Later, when I was with the gang, I watched Tom and John Perry from the Maniac Drifters play Russian roulette for a dollar a click. *Boom!* Tommy Perry blew his brains out in the park.

Another time, Big D., Honkey, and I were playing basketball at McPherson. Honkey took off for home. A few minutes later, we heard a distant boom. No one thought much about it. But in the park the next morning, people were talking: The Latin Kings had shot off Honkey's head. Honkey was a Gaylord in my set. The war was raging.

My parents had no idea what I was into. If they had known, they would have tore my ass up. Then the gang stuff would have been over, because I cared very much about what they thought. But I was doing okay in school, which made them happy. I treated them like a king and a queen when they were home. And when they weren't, I minded my sister and big brother.

I'm sure if we had lived in a black neighborhood, Mom and Dad would have worried more. But they got lax, because the neighborhood was predominately white and that was supposed to make it safe.

Of course, that made it unsafe for us. One Saturday, Kelly and a friend of his named Krutz were chased home by three white dudes who belonged to a gang called TJO, for Thorndale Jack Offs. The guys in TJO were like today's skinheads.

"We're going to hang you, nigger!" is what they shouted at Krutz and Kelly.

My sister tried to intervene. "Get away from my brother," she screamed at the two guys, with a metal poker in her hand.

When my homey Gary and I arrived, Janice told us, "Those guys just chased Kelly home. They say they're going to hang him."

"Yeah, we're going to hang you, too, nigger," one of them yelled at me.

"You know what?" I shouted back. "You done fucked with the right one, punk."

The TJOs were in their twenties. I wasn't even fourteen. But I snatched the poker from my sister and chased them down the street. Gary, who was fourteen, too, grabbed a bat from the porch and followed me. Now these white boys were running from *us*.

When one guy fell down, I started beating him with the poker. Gary was smacking him with the baseball bat. I had every intention of killing him.

"Eric, please don't kill him," Kelly cried, running down the street. "He ain't worth it. Don't kill him."

Just then, a carload of Latin Kings pulled up. They got out of the car with blackjacks and billyclubs and also started whacking the guy. He just lay there. Then we heard a police siren and beat it back to the house.

The next evening, some TJO guys drove past our house and threw a bomb on the porch. It was made out of gunpowder, bullets, and metal fragments. The words "KKK" and "nigger" were written on it. Luckily for us, the bomb fizzled out and did no real damage.

My parents thought some racists in the neighborhood were trying to run us out. I went along with that, knowing full well who had thrown the bomb and what I was going to do about it. That night, I went down the block to Pierce Grade School, where the boys from TJO hung out. "They stepped to my family," I told one of their leaders. "I ain't having it. I want the guy who threw that bomb to come up, so me and him can box. Heads up."

"Well, he doesn't want to box you," the leader said. "We didn't know it was your family."

I knew he was lying. Later, when I told my cousin Cornbread, he said, "Man, fuck this. This ain't goin' pass."

"I ain't lookin' to get nobody but the boy who did this," I told him. "This is personal. And if somebody from TJO wants to come step to it after that, then we'll take that whole mob out."

The next Monday at school, some members of the Basement Boys and the Gaylords approached me and said, "Man, why you shoot everybody up?" they asked.

"Hold on," I said. "I didn't shoot nobody."

But I was thinking it had to be Cornbread who had acted. I went back to TJO. They practically ran Senn High School, where my sister was a student. Senn had race riots almost every day. If the black kids got to school late, the white kids wouldn't let them inside. Then once they were in, the gang wouldn't let them out. I told one of the leaders, "Here's a list of my family members. If you fuck with them, it's back on." My sister and cousin never had another problem at Senn.

Now I was starting to believe in the power I was getting off the street. *I* was becoming that power. Giving up that sense of power is the hardest part of separating from the gang. I had to damn near lose my life in order to leave my gang. When you're thirteen, you don't think you can die. But I almost did. It was the best thing that ever happened to me.

I had been with the gang for over a year but I was never really out of control. For one thing, the older guys in the gang monitored what the younger ones did. And then there was no way I could let my parents know what I was into. A lot of us in the organization were like that. We did one thing on the street and another when we got home.

That Sunday in May 1974, six of us gangbangers headed to the show at the Uptown Theater to see Bruce Lee's *Return of the Dragon*. The Uptown was where Bugsy Malone and Al Capone once went to see concerts. On this day, it was the meeting place for the new Chicago mobsters. The Latin Eagles, all Puerto Rican boys, were already there. So were some friends of mine from the Latin Kings. Our group was a mixture of Vice Lords and Gaylords; the brothers and the Puerto Ricans were Vice Lords and the white boys were Gaylords. When we walked in, the Eagles were already ex-changing sharp words with the Kings. Immediately they shifted their attention to us, saying that we couldn't enter the theater. Of course, we weren't going to hear that.

As I started into the inner lobby, this Puerto Rican guy from the Eagles tried to stop me. He was about 5'8", thin, the playboy type. I just looked at him as if to say, "You gotta be a crazy fool" and walked by.

Then Casanova made the mistake of getting in my face. "Yo, I'm talking to you," he said. "You got about a minute to get up out of this show."

I was with my boys and he was with his boys and we were both out to see who could piss the farthest. I looked at him and said, "I'm walking over there and getting me some popcorn and some Raisinettes."

As I walked by, I saw this cute Puerto Rican girl standing next to him. She had wavy hair and was wearing red lipstick. I decided to twist the knife on him just like he'd tried to twist it on me. "Hey, baby, how you doin'?"

She dropped her head. He shot her a look. "I don't know him," she told Casanova. "I don't know why he's talking to me."

Casanova confronted me in the popcorn line. "You better get up out of here," he said for the second time.

I didn't know this guy from the Man in the Moon, but since I was breaking his balls by talking to his girl, I was going to keep it up. I walked past him and right up to her. "Hey, baby," I said. "Look, why don't you take your little brother home. Then you and me can get together."

That did it. The boy snapped. He started shouting about not dis-respecting his woman and how he was going to get me. Right then, I knew I had gone too far. If someone had hollered like that at my sister, my mama, my little woman, I would have felt the same way. But all I said to him was, "Look, you better get up out of my face. I don't know who you think you're talking to."

My boys were geeking me up. "Did you tell him where we come from, man?" one said.

"I was just about to tell that punk where we come from." With my face inches from his, I looked Casanova dead in the eyes. "Look, Joe, you got a problem with me, I'll be sitting in the front row. You get enough heart, come on in and find me."

I got my popcorn and started to walk into the theater when the conversation turned high-tech. I heard Casanova say to his girl, *"Mira, Negra."*

I stopped and looked back. *"Mira, Negra,"* he repeated. *"Deme la pistola."* The girl reached into her purse, took out a gun, and handed it to him.

*Boom!* He'd fired. As the bullet hit my stomach, I thought, *I can't believe he's shooting me. We were just bullshitting.*

Then I felt the pain. My teeth began to rattle and my knees buckled. Parents started to grab their kids and run from the theater. All the while my heart was racing. The gang members broke and ran. As far as I knew, there were only two people in the room—me and the man with the gun. I thought, *He wants to kill me.*

Just then, a brother from the Latin Kings, Reuben the Cuban, grabbed me and started to pull me toward the lobby's emergency exit door. Then Oscar, another Latin King, was knocked to the ground. Reuben ran to help him, while I hobbled over toward the door. As I pushed the lever to open it, I heard the crack of the gun and felt a sharp pain in the back of my calf.

When you're shot, you think, *I can't believe this is happening to me.* You feel so helpless. At that moment, I wished I had a gun. I wished I could have run. What I wished more than anything was that I had never gotten into that stupid argument.

As I stumbled toward home, I felt dizzy and scared. But it wasn't dying I was scared of—it was my mom. What was I going to tell her? . . .

Mom and Dad had always told me, "You must stand on your own, because you came in on your own and you're going to go out on your own."

Of course, I didn't listen to them. I thought my boys were always going to have my back. We were family. But when I got shot, I quickly found out who my real family was.

"I don't know what happened," I said when I somehow managed to make it home to my parents that day. "A van went by and I heard some shots and I was hit."

Dad loaded me into our car and drove me to Ravenswood Hospital. After all the pain, the running, the fear, I blacked out. The first thing I saw when I came to was my mama wailing, "Don't die. Don't die. Please, Lord, don't let my baby die."

I was terrified. Whenever my mom prayed that hard for somebody, the person died. *Oh, shit, this is real now,* I said to myself. "Don't pray for me, Mom. Whatever you do, don't pray for me like that."

"Please, Lord, let me die instead of my baby," she cried.

Lying in the ICU, I felt helpless as I watched my family around my bed, crying and wondering if I was going to make it. I started to say some of my own prayers. "Please, Lord, don't let my mama die," I said out loud. "Let *me* die. Who's going to take care of my brothers and sisters?"

Everything I had done up until then had been for *me,* about *me.* Now, for the first time, I was thinking about someone other than Eric. For the first time, I was asking myself, *What am I doing to my family? I did all this stupid shit for my boys—the boys who told me they would be there for me, who said they were family, and then they just left me.*

"Please, God, just give me one more chance," I pleaded softly. "I don't want to be in no gang no more. I won't do this again. Ever."

If you had asked me what I got shot with, I would have said, "A rocket." Actually, it was a .22. The bullets were old and fired from a distance. I was lucky. I was going to live.

My family soon found out everything that had happened. The boys were quick to tell the police I was gangbanging, and the officers paid a visit to my house and the hospital. My parents didn't say much about it to me, just that they'd thought I was more responsible and had better sense and that I should watch the company I keep. What else could they say? You're going to get killed? They knew I had learned my lesson.

My first week home, I didn't stray too far. I shot hoops at the garage or I stayed in the house. The next week, when I decided to venture farther, my parents' only words were, "Have a good time." I know that must have been tough for them. They were trying to act as if I had regained their trust and respect. I wasn't about to blow that. I had let my family down once; it wasn't going to happen a second time.

Even so, I had some unfinished business to take care of. I hadn't filed charges because like most guys in the gangs, I believed in taking care of things myself. Telling people I was out of the gang wasn't enough because I still had a reputation. So I needed some closure. The opportunity came about a month after the shooting. When I heard Casanova was going to be at a house party near Wrigley Field, I bought a gun on the street for $25, then waited for the right moment. I caught him on the back porch of his house, kissing his girlfriend.

"Please, don't shoot us," the girl said, weeping, when she looked up to find my pistol pointed at them. "Please, don't shoot us."

By street law, I was supposed to shoot the guy who shot me. "You didn't give me a break," I stated calmly. "But I'm going to give you a break. All I'm asking is for you to tell your boys that I'm out of this. If I was still in I would do you right now. But I'm going to give you something instead: your life. What you're going to give me is my freedom."

"No problem, no problem, no problem," Casanova kept saying.

I really had not planned to shoot them. The thing that scares me is I know that I would have if Casanova hadn't agreed to do what I asked or had tried to pull some macho shit. Fortunately, he didn't make a move as I walked away.

After I left them, I threw the gun in the sewer. This was either the beginning of my being a gangster big-time, or it was going to be the end.

It turned out to be the end. The Latin Eagles never gave me any problems, nor did my homeys. Red Dog, my former mentor, told me. "I seen your jump shot. That's your ticket. Being in this gang shit, you're only going to end up shooting heroin. Man, head on." I made it out.

Once I broke from the gang, school and basketball began to play a bigger role in my life. After three years of starting on the eighth-grade team at McPherson, I won basketball scholarships to three suburban prep schools and chose Loyola Academy, an all-boys school in wealthy Wilmette. Moms was happy because she didn't want me back in school with the boys, but I was miserable. Besides a ninety-minute commute each way, Loyola was just too far out of my reality. I told my mom I wanted to switch to the neighborhood school. She was obviously disappointed but let me transfer when I promised I would keep my grades up.

At Roald Amundsen High School, I was put into all honors classes. But I didn't want to be in honors. Being smart wasn't cool. Plus, I was the only black kid in most of my classes. In spite of myself, I received straight A's from then on. I wasn't going out of my way to make A's, but once I got interested in the courses, I had no trouble doing the work. The teachers also treated me like an adult, so I began to act like one. Soon I wanted to show off my intelligence. I found myself participating in discussions and even making friends with some of my classmates.

In sports, I was doing as well as I was in class. I was named to the high school All-American teams in basketball and football, and by senior year I had dozens of calls from colleges and universities inviting me to visit their campuses. As I traveled around the country, my parents seemed overwhelmed by the attention I was getting. Even if they had wanted to send me to these schools, they wouldn't have known how. I was going places they had never been.

I settled on Iowa State, but after a year transferred to Houston, where I played basketball with Michael Young, Clyde Drexler, and Hakeem Olajuwaun. In 1982, my senior year, we made it to the Final Four of the NCAA tournament. I couldn't wait for it to happen, and when it did, I couldn't believe it. I thought back to all those jump shots I'd made, all the snow I'd shoveled off the playground basketball court, all those gloves I'd cut at the fingertips so I could play through winter. . . .

Then when we lost the semifinal game against the University of North Carolina, a team that had Sam Perkins, James Worthy, and a very young Michael Jordan, I told myself, "It's over." Playing in the Final Four had been my NBA. It was time for me to get a job and put my psychology degree to use.

The summer before Houston, I had taken the Chicago police test, at my mom's urging. At the start of my senior year, I was asked to attend the Police Academy. "Nah, they're shooting police up there," I told Mom, laughing. "And what am I going to tell my homeys if I become the police? No way, I'm too close to finishing college."

After college, I still wasn't ready to join Chicago's finest. I accepted an offer to play professional basketball for the Killester Cats in Ireland. In one year, I averaged thirty points a game and became the leading scorer in the league, but I was tired of basketball. I took my $25,000 salary and returned to Chicago.

I wasn't home two days when another letter from the Chicago police arrived, again asking me to attend the Academy. About the same time, the Dallas Cowboys invited me to camp. I figured I could do both. If I got cut from the Cowboys, I would still have a police job to come back to.

To get ready for camp, I threw myself into the Academy's physical training regime. I started making friends. I still wasn't sure I'd be back the next week, but I was beginning to get more excited about being a police officer.

Meanwhile, I was on top of the world because my wife, Carol, was expecting our first child. We had met three years earlier at a Chicago nightclub and two years later, in August 1984, we got married in City Hall. Soon after, Carol was pregnant. Everything was going so well. I felt unstoppable.

Our daughter Erica was born on August 5, 1985, with a congenital heart defect, something they had not detected during my wife's pregnancy. Every day we sat next to Erica's crib, hoping and praying we could take her home. She hung on for a month. Then her heart just gave out.

There were no tears at first, only anger. Although my classmates from the Academy showed up at her funeral, the police department clergy offered their assistance, and my family rallied around me, I felt like I was alone. I was mad when people asked me what the problem was and mad when they didn't ask. Mostly, I was furious with God, because God had let me down. The death of a child is one of the toughest things any human being can go through. It still remains the worst thing that has ever happened to me. I thought I'd been through enough hard times and had earned something better now. After all, I had stopped gangbanging, I had gone to college, I played in the Final Four.

Eventually, I realized I was becoming as arrogant as I had been before I got shot. My baby dying was God's way of telling me to start living my life right again.

For the first time in my whole life, I began to cry. I had grown up thinking if someone hits you, you hit him back. If he's bigger than you, then pick something up to hit him. But don't cry, no matter what. I had suppressed all my feelings, until after a while, I didn't have any feelings. When I started to cry over losing my baby, I knew I was going to get better.

I rediscovered my faith by becoming a Muslim. Back when I was in Houston, I used to have long discussions with Hakeem about Islam. He told me the word *Islam* means peace. I sure needed some of that. When I began to pray and attend mosque, I found peace not only with myself but with God.

This changed the way I did everything, including police work. One of the pillars of Islam is to do your duties to humankind. To me, being a policeman is the ultimate duty. I actually volunteered to come to Cabrini in 1986, a year after I got on the job. I thought, *Just let me help where I can help.*

Now I feel like I do God's work every day. For a long time after converting to Islam, I wanted to be an Iman or prayer leader. Then I realized I'm *already* a prayer leader, only I go to the projects every day and give God's teachings in a way that the people there can understand them. Instead of a robe and kuffie, I wear blue jeans, tennis shoes, and a baseball cap. Instead of preaching the Koran, I tutor children and share my knowledge with parents on how to raise their children. I give a little boy a dollar so he can get himself something to eat instead of having to knock somebody in the head for it. I set up and hold together peace treaties so children and the elderly can go to school and to the supermarket. Sometimes I make an arrest as part of that service, though a lot of times I think that's the easy way out. Most people I arrest are really crying out for help, so I respond by trying to find them a job, a drug and alcohol clinic, or a GED program—something that answers their cry and gives them another chance. And when it comes time to knock on a mother's door and tell her about her son or daughter, I know what that feels like, too. I don't tell her my whole story. I just let her know that I understand.

Most of all I understand the kids, because I've been where they've been. Take the case of Antoine. When I first spotted Antoine, he was out chasing a group of other boys. Suddenly, he stopped and just opened fire. Bang. Bang. Bang. Antoine, all of fourteen himself, was shooting at small kids, women, everybody. I told him to put the gun down. He turned and started shooting at me. My sergeant and I fired back. As my sergeant stopped to reload, Antoine aimed his gun at him. So I shot him in the leg. Subsequently, when we went to court, the judge let Antoine go, saying that he had suffered enough even though he had shot at a police officer. *What will this boy learn about the value of life?* I thought. I decided it was up to me to teach him. I started by showing Antoine that I was concerned about him, and wanted to be involved in his life. I told him, "You've just adopted a big brother." I hounded him about going to rehab for his leg. Every time I saw him with his guys, I threatened to lock all of them up. I told his mama that she needed to spend more time with him and keep track of where he was. I made sure he was in school. Even if these actions sometimes seemed more like annoyances than demonstrations of love, Antoine got the message—I cared enough to come down on him, and lift him up. I had big expectations for him. Now Antoine has his high school diploma and has moved out of Cabrini.

Reading my own story like this in black and white, my first impression is, "Man, I had a loser life." But I've never experienced it that way. By expecting the best from life and from myself, I've managed to achieve my dreams. I try to share those dreams and expectations with others.

# 4: Give

# Something Back

*I was blessed by God to be raised by my grandmother.*
—JAMES MARTIN

The first time my mama got pregnant, she was fourteen. My mother, Odessa, and my father, James Martin, who was then eighteen, went to Iowa, where they could be married. My sister Darlene was born just after Mama's fifteenth birthday, and within a couple months, Mama was pregnant again. This time, the baby, James Kermit Martin III, was born with brain damage and lived only eight or nine days. By the end of that year, on December 16, 1960, I was born at Providence Hospital on the South Side of Chicago. Mama named me James Kermit Martin IV.

Not long after I was born, my father left and my mother just sort of lost it. She was seventeen, with two kids and a lousy husband who had just skipped out on her. When I was eight months old, my grandmother's sister, Aunt Lou, came to pick me up for the weekend from my mama's apartment in the Altgeld Gardens housing project. My mother was hanging out with a friend next door while I was running a fever so high Aunt Lou had to rush me to the county hospital. The doctors said I had double pneumonia and kept me in the hospital for the next eight weeks. By the time they released me, Mama was running wild in the streets. So her mother, Mrs. Estella McIntyre, took me and Darlene into her home in the Ida B. Wells housing project. My grandmother became the only parent I ever had.

My mother, meanwhile, was a little sex machine. After me, she had my brother Glenn, who also came to live with us, and later, my sister LaShawne and brothers Robert and Antawaun. In between LaShawne and Robert, she had another girl. The baby died in an ambulance on the way to the hospital.

Growing up, I learned everything I knew about my mother from the postcards I would get from all the places she was staying. Las Vegas. Canada. Los Angeles. She was definitely a free spirit. Every now and again, she would come see us at my grandmother's. Then, when I was eleven or twelve, Mama moved into the Ickes housing projects on State Street, where she raised LaShawne, Robert, and Antawaun. I started going to their house on weekends.

I knew something was wrong when every time I turned around she had a different man in the house. That's when I figured out my mama was a prostitute. There would be constant knocks at the door from people wanting to buy sex or drugs. Mama was both selling drugs and using them, too. She didn't care what she got high on, though heroin seemed to be her drug of choice.

Considering what my mama exposed me to, I suppose I could have become a dope dealer at a young age. But dope never attracted me, because I saw what it did to her. She couldn't take care of her kids, and she could barely take care of herself.

Somehow, though, she always managed to have a couple of trifling boyfriends around. When I was fourteen, there was this white dude named Bob, who used to cook for her and send her to rehab. He even got her to become a drug counselor for a while. We were all upset when she broke up with him. Then, there was a guy we thought for a long time was Antawaun's father, but we later found out his dad was some guy in the joint. As for Glenn, the only thing any of us knew about *his* father was that he was someone Mama met in Canada. "You ain't no real Martin," I used to tease and make him cry. My grandmother would tear up my butt for that.

Meanwhile, we kids never discussed the things my mother was doing. We were raised to respect her, even though the things she was doing in front of us were disrespectful. Also, we didn't bad-mouth family. My grandmother, especially, would never say anything hurtful about her baby. Odessa was her only child, which made us kids think Mama behaved that way because she was spoiled. All I knew was, my mother was lost for some reason.

My father was another mystery. As a child, I didn't remember him at all. The only thing I knew about James Martin II was that his mother also lived in Ida B. On Christmas Day, we would cross Madden Park to go to her house and open presents from our father. But we never saw him. Then, when I was twelve or thirteen, the presents stopped coming.

I suppose I could have hated my mother and father. I just didn't think about them. I never sat around and whined, "I don't have no mama; I don't have no daddy." Back then, most of my closest friends were being raised by single parents. I focused on my grandmother and my sisters and brothers. I focused on trying to do for me so I could make my life better. I couldn't pick my parents. God gave them to me. So, they became my role models—for how *not* to be.

I promised myself as a child that one day I would make it in life just so I could hear my mother and father proudly say, "That's my son." Then I would tell them, "No, I'm not. You didn't do anything. I'm Mrs. McIntyre's son. Mrs. McIntyre was my mother. Mrs. McIntyre was my father. She's who raised me. She's who was there for me."

My grandmother is the reason I'm where I am today. She was short and stout, with dark skin and wavy hair, and she was all business. Originally from Tutwiler, Mississippi, she and my grandfather, Steve McIntyre, moved to Chicago in 1948, when my mama was eight. Because he was a disabled veteran, the government gave them an apartment at Ida B. Wells. They were poor, but they tried to give Mama the best any poor child could have. My grandfather supplemented his disability pension by cutting hair, and my grandmother helped him.

I don't remember my grandfather much, because he died when

I was three. My grandmother supported herself on my grandfather's pension, and when we moved in, she took my father to court and won child support from him. He paid the state and the state paid us through Aid to Families with Dependent Children—or, as we used to call it, After Daddy Cut Out.

Though she didn't work, my grandmother was never one to sit around the house doing nothing. She joined all these school advisory councils and committees for school desegregation and public housing. She went to meetings around the state and got numerous awards for her service to Chicago public schools. She didn't have a college degree, but she knew what she believed in: "her" kids— and by that, she meant everybody's kids. Mr. Coretz, my principal at Doolittle West Grammar School, knew if he wanted to get rid of a bad teacher, all he had to do was tell my grandmother. She was a powerful woman and rose from the local council at Doolittle to the citywide council to the state council. She was my ace in the hole. I knew if I got in trouble, I had the ups: my grandmother.

But I didn't get into trouble because that meant I would have had to deal with her. I wasn't scared of the police growing up; I was scared of my grandmother. My grandmother did her own disciplining. She would hit us with the broom or her hand, or she would pull out the little belt she always kept in her purse. If we started clowning in a store, she'd pull that belt out and whip you on the spot. Or if we were at home, she'd tell us, "Go get the belt."

Then, too, we always had an extra belt hanging over our head if we got out of line, because my grandmother gave other adults permission to hit us too. She was so well known around Ida B. that anytime we did something wrong, we heard, "I'm going to tell Miss McIntyre," or "Ain't you Miss McIntyre's grandson?" Very early on, we learned that there were consequences for our actions.

My grandmother didn't care how big we were. "This is my house," she would tell us. "The only opinion in this house is mine. When you get an opinion, it's time for you to leave." I have always said my grandmother should have been running a jail somewhere. When we were tall enough to reach the sink, we were washing dishes. When we were tall enough to reach the ironing board, we were ironing our clothes. I didn't wear the best clothes growing up, and most of them were hand-me-downs, but they were always clean and pressed. My sister did all the cooking while Glenn and I had to clean the house, mop the hallways, and take care of the outside. By Saturday, the room Glenn and I shared had to be in order. On school days, we came straight home and did our homework before we went outside to play. And then we had to stay close enough to hear our names hollered from the porch.

We had some fun moments with our grandmother, too. I can remember plenty of occasions where we would sit down in front of the television to watch my grandmother's favorites, wrestling and horse racing. During those times, she would laugh and joke and even relax the rules for a while by letting us eat hot dogs and french fries in the living room.

My grandmother pushed respect and pride. Despite all the discipline and fear my grandmother instilled in us, we stayed good not because we would get a whipping, but because we didn't want to disrespect our house or community. We were proud of who we were and where we came from. My grandmother would tell us, "The projects weren't made for folks to be living in forever. It's for you to use as a stepping-stone. We may be living here now, but you should try to get out of this environment."

Even so, I didn't view where we lived negatively. I never hung my head in shame. If people asked me where I lived, I didn't say the projects. I said, "I live in Ida B." I lived in a community. I knew it was a housing project, but community is a feeling you have. Buildings don't make a neighborhood; the people *in* the buildings make a neighborhood. As long as you have love and support in your house, you have the basis of a good community.

I ask kids today, "How many of you live in the projects?" Most of them are too timid to raise their hands because they've bought into the negative stereotype of the projects. Not us. We were proud of who we were. I'm proud to say I was a project kid, if only to shatter that stereotype.

Of course, Ida B. Wells was a lot different when I was growing up. We lived in the same two-bedroom apartment our mama had grown up in, number 588 at 526 E. 37th Place. In front of our three-story building, we had grass and a peach tree my grandmother had planted. Because we lived on the first floor, we were responsible for keeping the ground level, the first flight of stairs, and the second level clean. As the oldest boy in the building, I ended up sweeping and mopping from the third floor down every Saturday. Then, I would go to the building next door, where this old lady named Miss Saunders lived, and sweep and mop her hallway for her. Afterward, I would do her grocery shopping and earn $3 or $4 for the full day's work. I was ten and already learning to hustle.

The Chicago Housing Authority (CHA) also ran the projects a lot differently then than it does today. Our apartments and buildings were inspected once a year. Our janitor, Mr. Levi, used to clean up the backyard and leave us the key to the basement where the incinerator and his equipment were. That way if a lightbulb needed replacing on one of the landings, we replaced it. We didn't wait for CHA to do anything. Nor were they policing our neighborhood. We did that.

Crime was never really a problem, though. For one thing, living in all-black Ida B. was like having one big family. I knew everybody from my block to two blocks down in any direction. If I didn't know people by name, I knew where they lived. How many people living in these expensive high-rise buildings on Lake Shore Drive can name even five of their neighbors?

A lot of our neighbors were members of the Black Panthers. The party was big in Ida B. in the sixties. I remember a lot of days I was fed by the Panthers' free breakfast program. They weren't preaching "hate white folks" or any of that craziness. They were telling us to stand up and be strong, to take pride in who we were and honor and protect our community. They taught us the value of education and family. And we soaked it all up.

There were gangs then, too. I knew all the gang members and the dope sellers, because we'd grown up together. My cousin Stanley was on the Goon Squad, a branch of the Disciples. I had friends who were Stones and some who were Vice Lords. And a lot of people in Ida B. looked up to the El Rukuns, because of their strong Muslim beliefs and self-discipline. Since they controlled the drug trade in Ida B., they kept down a lot of nonsense. There was no gangbanging or turf wars.

I, myself, never had any interest in joining a gang. My cousin Steve, who was about ten years older than me, was a Stone. Police were always raiding his house and coming up with guns and drugs. Steve was forever going to jail, and his mother, Miss Hattie Mae, was forever crying. I looked forward to a better life. My role models became my cousin Sonny, Uncle John, the Black Panthers, and my grandmother—all people working hard for themselves and their community.

By age fourteen, I was no longer a child. What little childhood I had left after witnessing my mother's antics and being the oldest male in the household was over when I started working and giving my grandmother money for rent.

Though I really didn't like working as a fourteen-year-old, it never occurred to me to be anything but responsible. Seeing all the things my grandmother did for us, how she sacrificed, how my Aunt Lou and Uncle Sam gave so much, made me feel like I should try to help myself and my family too. My grandmother hadn't had to take us in but I was grateful that she had. Sometimes when she got really mad at us, she would start yelling about how much she'd given up to take care of us. Whenever she would say those things, I always worried she might send us back to Mama's.

Still, there were times I got tired of being the "father" of the family. "I'm a kid," I wanted to shout. I should have been able to go to the adults in my life when I needed help, but I couldn't. If I had problems, I didn't talk about them. Sharing them with my mother and father was out of the question. My grandmother, who I felt would listen, was always so busy and, in her fifties, could only do so much. So I kept everything to myself. I figured out my problems on my own. At a young age, I learned that I couldn't put my life in anyone else's hands. I was going to have to depend on myself.

My first job was emptying the incinerators at school during lunch period. Every day, I went back to class smelling like garbage, until somebody pointed out that it might be unsafe for a kid to be around so much fire and smoke, and I was moved to the school office. Then, the summer before my sophomore year, I became a stock clerk at Jewel Food Store and remained there until I graduated.

Working allowed me to get some of the stuff my friends had, like minibikes or floor-model TVs. Knowing my grandmother didn't have much money to spend, I wasn't going to burden her by saying "I really want this, I really want that." If I wanted something, I was going to have to get it on my own.

So I bought my own everything. In a way, it was a good feeling, being able to do that. Some kids had to wait on their mamas to buy them stuff. I didn't ask anybody for anything. I did just what my grandmother always taught me: Strive for things, then go out and get them yourself. If I wanted a minibike after I paid my portion of the rent, no one could say anything.

A lot of my money went toward my growing interest in music. Deejaying house parties became my hustle in high school. I was majoring in electronics at Dunbar Technical High School and spending my check from the Jewel on records and sound equipment.

At school, I avoided trouble. I was into books, sports, and music. Getting an education and trying to make something out of myself—these were more important than dating and sex. Like most boys, I thought about sex, but I knew one slip could get a girl pregnant and I didn't want any of those problems.

Dunbar's ROTC had the coldest drum and bugle corps around, and I wanted to be a part of that. Also, ever since I was a kid, I had been thinking about joining the military. A few of my uncles had served in the army and a couple of my cousins were in the navy and air force. All of them were my role models, along with the Black Panthers and the black male leaders I read about in history books, such as Malcolm X and Dr. King. I knew the military could give me direction and structure. And I knew the army couldn't be worse than living with my grandmother.

So I started out as a private in ROTC, and by my senior year I was named lieutenant colonel, the number-one position in ROTC. I was in charge of the entire corps.

My grandmother had taught us to think big. That meant if we wanted to work in a kitchen, we shouldn't be the cook but the one who runs the show. "Don't aim to be the man on the bottom," she would say. "Try to be the man on top." So I applied to the United

States Military Academy at West Point. I was turned down. Apparently, although I was making A's and B's, the education offered by the Chicago public schools was not up to West Point's standards.

Meanwhile, at one of her state meetings, my grandmother struck up a conversation with a woman about how I had been turned down by West Point. It just so happened that this woman's husband worked in the USMA admission office. She told my grandmother about the United States Military Academy Prep School in Fort Monmouth, New Jersey. Less than a week after I graduated from Dunbar in June 1979, I was on my way there. Toward the end of my year at prep school, I applied to my state congressmen, Adlai Stevenson and Percy Stewart, for a nomination to USMA. They both gave me one. I was finally headed for West Point.

There's a lot of history at West Point and I was honored to be a part of it. Of course, there were some people who didn't feel I and other blacks belonged there, but West Point did not condone racism. I also arrived in the fall of 1980, the year after female cadets were first accepted. That made it a lot easier for blacks, since women were now catching all the hell we used to get. But, we knew that if it wasn't for them, we would still be at the bottom.

People make a big deal over West Point's discipline, but to me it was a joke compared to my grandmother's regime. To me, the hardest thing was learning to eat at the dining table using the proper drill. We had to sit ramrod straight, at a certain distance from the table, with our feet flat, our expressions fixed, and our eyes on the table. We had duties to perform before we could eat. There was also a proper way to eat. We could not cut a portion of our food wider than our fork. And when we put it in our mouths, we had to place our silverware on the plates, put our hands in our laps, and then chew. We had four chews to swallow each bite. As strange as it seemed, the point of the whole exercise was to teach us how to eat while carrying on a conversation. But during the first two weeks of getting used to that, nobody was eating seconds or dessert.

Being able to swim was a requirement for graduation. So, one day, I just showed up for the swim test. I stood last in line at one end of this Olympic-size swimming pool, not knowing how deep it was. "Martin, you're next." I jumped in and splashed my way through the pool until I was about three feet from the end. Suddenly, I realized, "I can't swim." I started to go under and a couple guys jumped in to save me. Later, they were like, "Man, you crazy." I just cracked up. To me it was a good experience. It's like I tell kids today: Anything you put your mind to, you can do. It's when you doubt yourself that you can't do it.

West Point was cool. But there were times I got real homesick, especially when I would visit my grandmother and see how much she was struggling to make ends meet. Glenn was having a rough time in high school and losing direction. Darlene was still living at home but now had two kids. And Robert had moved from my mama's house to my aunt's and finally into a boys' home. I hated that I wasn't there to help them.

The decision to leave after my freshman year was easy. Going to West Point had been my dream, but suddenly it didn't seem as important to me as helping my family. My grandmother really wanted me to stay. Looking back on the decision now, I can't say I regret it. Sure, I would have liked to graduate from West Point, but I could never replace my family or the things I do for them. In my life, my family always comes first. So I returned to Ida B. and got my job back at the Jewel store.

At home, I gave Darlene guidance and tutored Glenn. I was also helping my grandmother with the finances. Before long, I was father of the household again, especially for my brother Robert. Robert had a real bad temper. He would hit you if you touched him or pushed him. Once, when he was young, he got into a fight with another boy. He beat him up, then he grabbed a bottle, broke it, and cut the kid. Robert had so much rage. He would actually foam at the mouth. When he threw tantrums, he would grab a knife and chase us. I was the only one who could calm him down.

I don't know where all that anger and hostility came from. Maybe Robert felt my mother didn't love him the same way she loved her other kids because she had sent him at age six to live with Aunt Lou. By fourteen, he was too uncontrollable for my aunt. She sent him to Lawrence Hall School for Boys, a group home in Chicago for disruptive students. On family days at Lawrence Hall, I would be there for Robert. I represented the family. If a teacher or principal needed to see his parent, I went then, too. Even with psychiatrists and counselors to help him twenty-four hours a day, he was still a terror his first couple of years and was accused of setting a fire. It took four strong guys to tackle him when he got out of hand.

Finally, Robert got involved in athletics, and his temperament seemed to improve. One day, he came over to Ida B. to play basketball with me, Glenn, and another dude. The dude fouled him real hard. Glenn and I looked at each other. *Oh, no, he's going to start fighting,* I thought. Instead, Robert got up and started playing again. "Man," I said to Glenn, "he's changed."

Not quite six months after I came home, my grandmother, who was then sixty, went to the doctor for a checkup. He told her she should cut down on smoking, but otherwise she was in good health. She and I talked about her checkup briefly, then I left. I was still mad at her about an argument we'd had the day before. That night, my grandmother went to sleep and never woke up again.

I was devastated. Not only had I lost the person closest to me, but I couldn't help but feel that it was my fault. Maybe if we hadn't gotten into that stupid argument, which I can't even remember, my grandmother would not have had a heart attack and she would still be here today. Or if I had known that I would never talk to her again, I could have told her, "I'm sorry for being a jerk." I could have said how much I loved her and appreciated what she had done for my family and me. She was my torch in life. She taught me my values and gave me direction. She sacrificed her life for me.

For years, I blamed myself for my grandmother's death. I never talked about it until six years later. Just thinking about it still bothers me now. I feel like a lot of things I do today, whether it's caring for my family, helping other people, or just carrying myself a certain way, I do for her, to make up for what I wasn't able to tell her, in hopes that she might see me and be proud. My grandmother lived her whole life giving to other people, especially those less fortunate. The least I can do is give back some of what she gave to me.

Before she died, my grandmother encouraged me to take the police test. I was still working at Jewel but definitely wasn't going to make a career out of it. I wanted to give back to my community the way my grandmother had. Becoming a police officer seemed one of the best ways to do that. Not only was it service-oriented, but I was comfortable with a military structure. As a police officer, I could make sure poor folks like me got decent police service, something that was lacking when I was growing up in the projects. I took the test in 1982, and, after working at Jewel for three more years and after a police hiring freeze ended, I was approved to attend the Police Academy.

When I took the job, I told everybody in the family, "I'm going to allow you to get in trouble once, and I'll do everything I can to help you. After the first time, you're on your own, because then it's no longer a mistake. You've chosen crime as your occupation."

Robert and Antawaun seemed to be making that choice. Antawaun is the hard-core, gangbanging gunslinger of the family. He's a super streetwise brother. I didn't realize how bad he was until he got a little bit older, because he acted one way at our house and totally different at Mama's. When he was with her, he was gangbanging. The gang was his everyday family, while Mama was either out doing her thing or home drunk. But, if she needed help, Antawaun was always there, by her side. Sometimes he'd even have to pull her, drunk, out of the hallways. Meanwhile, she defended him, no matter what he did. That may be one reason he turned out so bad.

I was still doing my first year of police training the first time Antawaun got arrested. He was fourteen. He had cussed out Mama, painted somebody's door, and done some other juvenile nonsense. When I picked him up, I said, "Twaun, this is your first time." Then, in his freshman year, he got kicked out of school for knocking out a woman and robbing her—right inside the school. He was told he could never attend another school in Chicago. I went to court with him, and the judge gave him a year's probation. With three weeks left on his probation, he got locked up again, this time for allegedly taking a leather jacket off some dude. He told the guy to run, then shot at him for the heck of it. Luckily, he missed. When my mama asked for money to pay Twaun's attorney, I told her, "I'm not giving you a dime."

Robert's first chance came his senior year at Lawrence Hall. One of his friends was house-sitting for this rich dude and decided to take some stuff from the house, including some Krugerands and a Fiat car. Because the friend couldn't drive a stick, he called Robert. I ended up going to court with him, and he got off with probation. Then he got locked up for another robbery. My mother again asked me for money for a lawyer. "When he did that last robbery," I said to her, "I told him he was on his own. I'm not giving him a dime for an attorney or anything else. Those are *your* sons. They're only my brothers."

After he graduated from Lawrence Hall, Robert seemed to calm down. He always kept a job, sometimes two and three. While he might have called himself a gang member, he wasn't actively gang-banging. He was doing all right until about two years ago, when he let his emotions get the better of him.

Robert bought a used Chevy Blazer from this young man. He still owed him money, but it turned out the truck needed a whole new engine, so he told the dude he wasn't going to pay him the rest. The young man came over to Robert's house while Robert was at work and, according to his wife, pushed her around. That was all it took for Robert to get fired up.

At the time, Antawaun was living with Robert and staying out of trouble. Robert woke him up in the middle of the night and said, "Come on with me." The two of them left with a sawed-off shotgun and a pit bull. First they went looking for the man at his girlfriend's house. Then they went to his mother's house. Finally, they got the address where he stayed and kicked the door in. The guy woke up and fired a gun sitting by his bed. Two shots hit Antawaun in the chest and the stomach. Antawaun fired the shotgun at the man, missed, then ran out to the alley. As soon as the first shots were fired, Robert got in his Blazer and drove off. Then he remembered Antawaun and drove back to get him.

Antawaun nearly died. All of us crowded around his hospital bed. Even LaShawne flew in from Germany, where she was stationed in the army. When Twaun finally woke up after several operations, he was hooked up to tubes, machines, and a colostomy bag. His hands were also handcuffed to the sides of the bed.

"What's these?" he asked, looking at the cuffs. "I'm the victim."

Before they went to the hospital, Antawaun and Robert came up with a story. Robert told the police that Antawaun was at an El station when he got into it with some Disciples who tried to rob him. The boys shot Antawaun, and he managed to page Robert to come get him. Considering Antawaun is a pretty streetwise brother with gang tattoos and all, the story is pretty believable. But when the police checked it out, they found no blood at the El station nor any 911 calls from there. So they went back to Robert. After more questioning, he came clean.

Now they're both in Graham Correctional Center, about four hours away from Chicago. Antawaun is serving fifteen years and Robert, eight, for home invasion, attempted murder, armed violence, and unlawful use of a weapon by a felon. I didn't waste my time going to visit them when they were held in the County. I didn't even go to their court hearings. But since they moved to Graham, I write and send them money. I understand their plight. I was raised by my grandmother. They were raised by my mother. It shows in where they've ended up. I don't love them any less, so I'm still going to help them when I can.

It's sad to say, but I think most black families in America can relate to my situation, since many of them have a relative who is a member of a street gang or serving time in the penitentiary. There's a rule that officers are prohibited from associating with known felons. But that would mean cutting off my own family, something I could never do. Robert and Antawaun will always be my family, no matter what.

I have seen much more of my father since I returned to Chicago. He acts all proud of me now. "That's my son," he tells people. "He's a policeman." I don't say anything. I just look at him, knowing he didn't do a damn thing to make me a Chicago police officer. But when he got married recently, I was the best man at his wedding. In fact, all the Martin boys were standing up there. My father will not deny his kids. He's too proud of us. His thing was to create families and just move on—leave the child-rearing for someone else. But now I understand he always did love us; he just didn't know how to show it.

In the last five years, I've learned more about my parents than I ever knew in all my childhood. I found out my mama robbed banks, forged checks, shot people, and served time in Detroit, Toronto, and Vegas. I also learned that her father molested her when she was a little girl. For so long, I blamed my mother's crazy ways on her being spoiled. Now I understand a little better why she was so messed up. No kid deserves to be abused. Still, that didn't change how I thought of her. My grandmother, Mrs. McIntyre, will always remain my only mother.

I haven't forgotten the promise I made as a child to get back at my parents. But now that they've seen how I turned out, what's more important than the promise itself is what it's pushed me to do. Not only have I made a life to be proud of, but I've made a life of helping others to do the same. I owe it all to my grandmother.

# 5: Be a Ray
# of Hope

*I always wanted to be a policeman when I grew up. I loved the noise and flashing lights of the police cars. When the policemen got out of their cars, people stopped whatever they were doing and listened. To me, that seemed like the job to have.*

—RANDY HOLCOMB

When I was five years old, I had my first encounter with the Chicago police. I was in kindergarten at St. Michael's Catholic School on the North Side. School had just let out and my brother Monroe, who was in second grade, and my sister Rena, who was in fourth, were walking me home as usual. We lived at North Avenue and Larabee, only four blocks from St. Michael's. But to get to Larabee, we had to cross Ogden Avenue, a busy intersection where there was always a police officer on the corner.

The officer on the corner was a typical Irish cop, a big, white-haired guy with a thick mustache. He was real friendly, and we spoke to him every day. As always, we waited for him to tell us to cross the street. But on that day, for some reason, his gun caught my eye.

Like most young boys, I was fascinated with guns. I pointed my index finger toward the gun. "Officer," I asked softly, "is that gun real?"

He never heard my question. At that moment Monroe yelled out, "Don't you touch that!"

Before I knew it, the officer had swung around and slapped me hard across the face. At first, I was too stunned to cry. Then reality flooded back as I heard my sister saying, "Ooooh, I'm going to tell."

The sting of the slap was quickly forgotten. I couldn't think of anything except the fact that I was going to get a whipping. For all the times I might have been bad and didn't get caught, now I had done nothing and was fixing to get it.

My sister and brother took off running toward the house, just three buildings from the corner of Larabee. I knew I had to get there before they did. But I was the smallest one and it was a struggle just to keep up. Tears rolled down my cheeks. My sister's words were like a bad song ringing in my ear: "I'm going to tell. I'm going to tell."

We lived on top of a Laundromat. Rena and Monroe flew up the stairs, leaving me at the landing. I could hear my sister talking to my mom as soon as she got in the door. "The police officer slapped Randy."

Now, to my parents, who came up from the South to find jobs in Chicago, the very fact that you got slapped by a police officer meant in their minds that you must have done something bad. My fate was sealed. With a five-year-old's vocabulary, I stumbled and stammered between sobs but couldn't find a way to tell my mother what had really happened.

Mom wasn't hearing any of it anyway. "I'm going to tell your father," she said. "You can lie to me, but you won't lie to him."

I was really crying now. Mom said, "Go change out of your school clothes."

When my father came home, I knew there was no use trying to explain to him what had happened. He was the kind of father you spoke to only when he spoke to you. After he whipped me, he told me to apologize to the officer the next day.

"That's all right, kid," the officer said when I told him I was sorry.

I never spoke to him again. My brothers and sisters would say hello, but I kept to myself. He remained on the corner for about a year before another officer took his place. I didn't speak to that one either. I just stepped back from the police completely. But I never forgot my dream of becoming a police officer.

I did have one question, though: Why? Why did the officer slap me for something I didn't do? The fact that he was white never entered my mind. I was around white people all the time. I lived next to them, went to school with them, played with them. I think I was more surprised that an older person had hit me. Usually older people in the neighborhood would threaten to tell your father if they caught you doing something wrong, or they might drag you home by the scruff of the neck and explain what had happened to your parents. This guy had slapped me—and made me get a whipping. I knew one thing for certain: It wasn't fair.

I was born in 1957, on the North Side of Chicago, the sixth of my parents' children. My daddy, Monroe Holcomb, was from Darnell, Louisiana, and my mom, Bertha, was raised in Shreveport. They met and married in Chicago. They had eleven children, with seventeen years between the oldest and the youngest. I was the man in the middle, with three brothers younger and three brothers older than me.

We lived above a Laundromat owned by a Greek couple. When we moved in, there was only one other black family in the neighborhood. We were almost your typical American family. My mother didn't work as long as we were living on the North Side. She got us up in the morning, made sure we ate and were dressed for school, packed our lunch boxes, then sent us off to the Catholic school. When we got home at 2:30, she always had dinner prepared. We ate, studied, and went to bed by eight. There was no watching TV.

My father worked hard as a plasterer for a construction company. He had an iron hand. When he came home from work, he didn't laugh or joke with us. One of the few times he would smile was while watching us play sports, which he made us do together. We knew not to bother Daddy and definitely not to say anything smart to him. Seen but not heard. Speak only when spoken to. My father lived by those mottos. If I even thought about talking to him, I started crying. I figured whatever I told him he was going to whip me for it. That was the kind of fear he instilled in us.

He also had a crazy way of disciplining us. If he whipped one, he whipped us all. When one of us would ask, "What am I getting a whipping for?" he would say, "Well, so-and-so messed up and you should have been watching him." Once, when I told on Monroe, Daddy whipped everybody, and then turned to me: "I'm going to whip you for telling on your brother." He wanted us to stick together no matter what, yet never lie to him.

Daddy was a strong, proud black man who believed in supporting his family. "Your job is to go to school and be obedient and well-mannered," Daddy used to say. When people saw us on the street, they could point us out: "That's one of those Holcombs." We never got smart with older people. We always said "Sir" and "Ma'am." It made my father proud to know we were all good kids.

David, my oldest brother, was the exception. He had a natural talent for drawing and boxing, but he got in so much trouble all the time. In eighth grade, David got kicked out of St. Michael's for fighting everybody, including the nuns. He never went back to school. At sixteen, he got married, moved into Cabrini-Green, and became the leader of one of the factions of the Black Stone Rangers. At eighteen, he went to jail for murder. But he didn't do it. David ended up beating the rap, but it took $7,000 or $8,000 of Daddy's money. Even so, no matter what David did, my father always stayed in his corner.

Eventually, David stopped all the gangbanging, but, just like a gunfighter in the Wild West, he couldn't shake his reputation. After having had so many people beaten, stabbed, and shot, he always had guys chasing him. One night, at a bar, he was stabbed eight times and left for dead. He survived. Another time, he was shot three or four times at close range. Once again, we thought he was dead, but he survived. Finally, in his thirties, David moved back into the house with us. It wasn't a bullet that caught up with him, but all the drinking he had done. In 1990, he died from cirrhosis of the liver at age forty-three.

Unlike David, I never liked to fight, probably because I was so skinny growing up. My family nicknamed me "Smiley," because I smiled so much. Once, while working with my father, this woman asked me my name. I was too shy to say it out loud. "We call him Smiley," one of my brothers interjected. So she started calling me Smiley. Later, my father took me aside and said, "Look, you've got to stop smiling so much if you want people to take you more serious."

Growing up, I always felt like what I did wasn't good enough. I was the black sheep of the family. Unlike my brothers, I didn't have light brown skin or hair good enough to make into a Jackson Five afro. They all seemed to have some talent or skill or characteristic that made them better. Monroe was big and strong, Allan was real smart, David was an artist and a gangster. My three younger brothers had girls all over them. I felt like I had none of those things. So I was always trying to outdo them and show everyone that I was just as good as they were.

For a long time, I excelled in school. Then I got into sports. I used to watch this Hispanic dude named Gabriel. He wanted to run track, but there was no track team at Precious Blood, the school I went to when my family moved to the West Side, so he ran along the streets of Chicago. I thought running was the key to being in shape, so I started running around the house. Eventually, I began running around the block. None of the neighborhood kids bothered me. Back then, if you were an athlete, people thought you were trying to make something of yourself. Gangs would refuse to let you join up because they were hoping you would make it as an athlete. I kept running, then I started playing basketball after school on the blacktop. Soon I was one of the tallest guys out there and playing with the big boys from the projects.

During the summers, I worked with my father, who had started his own paint and plaster business. He would always get family to work with him before asking anyone else. In fact, he used to joke that he had a son to help him for every day of the week.

One night, the summer before my senior year, I was coming back from a job with Daddy. We had worked nearly eleven hours on a North Side condo, and I was covered with plaster. I was looking forward to a hot bath and one of Mom's home-cooked meals. As I unloaded the station wagon, Larry and John, two friends from the neighborhood, stopped by and said, "Let's go play some ball."

The sun was starting to set. If I showered and put on fresh clothes, I knew I would be in for the night. So I decided to go in my dirty jeans, workshirt, and boots. We were on the court at Precious Blood Grade School when we heard police sirens. Several police cars were racing up Congress toward the El station at Western Avenue. "Come on," Larry said, "let's see what's happening."

"Man, I ain't goin up there," I told him. Because of my upbringing, I was never one to hang out. I also wasn't too fond of the police. But the real reason I didn't want to go was because I knew I would see some girls. Here I was covered in plaster, my hands were dry and ashy, and the hat on my head was barely covering my wild afro. I didn't want them to think I was some kind of bum.

But Larry kept urging, "Come on, man," so the three of us headed over there.

Standing among the crowd of people at the El station, I felt someone tugging at me. I turned and saw a tall black police sergeant, with salt-and-pepper hair, holding on to my arm. I looked at him with surprise and snatched my arm away.

"Bring your ass on over here," he said, grabbing my arm again.

"Man, I ain't done nothing. I'm just coming off work," I said as he led me through the crowd and down a covered ramp to the El platform.

The ramp seemed like a mile long, and all I could see at the end were more police officers. My heart was racing but everything else slowed down. I could see a man lying on the ground. His leg was cut and bleeding. Other police officers were standing around him. The sergeant shouted, "Look out," and the officers parted. He pulled me up real close to the man.

"Hey, is he the one that cut you?" the sergeant asked him.

The man gave the sergeant a blank look. Later, I found out the victim spoke only Spanish.

"Yeah, you done it," the sergeant said, turning to me. "Handcuff him."

A couple officers grabbed me. I started to protest, "Wait a minute. The guy didn't say I done this."

The officers started muscling me. "Turn around." They led me back up the ramp, this time in handcuffs, and shoved me in the back of a police car.

"John," I called from the car window. "Run and tell my parents what's going on."

Just as he turned to walk away, the sergeant grabbed him. "Oh, you're with him, huh?" He handcuffed John and put him next to me in the car.

John started to get mad. "Man, what's going on?" he asked me.

"I don't know," I said. "Somebody down there got cut, and they're saying I done it."

John looked at me. "What they thinking? You just came from work. We were out playing ball."

As we were trying to make sense of the whole scene, I overheard the sergeant say, "Yeah, we got 'em. Take them over to the station and process them."

Two black officers got in the car. One of them said, "You might as well go ahead and confess."

"Confess to what?" I asked.

He turned around. "Look, I ain't got time for no bullshit. You know you done it. We got you. You're going to jail."

"I ain't confessing to nothing. I ain't done nothing. I ain't going to say I did anything. That ain't happening."

Then John said, "Hey, brother, let me talk to you—"

"Hold it." The officer cut him off. "I ain't your motherfuckin' brother."

"Look, don't even say nothing," I whispered to John. I knew enough not to hold a conversation with the police because they would try to use it against you.

"Yeah, keep your mouth shut," the officer said. "Because the only thing that's going to beat you to this station is the front of this police car." The officers cracked up. John and I remained quiet for the rest of the ride.

They searched us in a small office where we were handcuffed to a steel ring attached to the wall. Of course, they didn't find anything. One of the officers started talking about the way I looked. "He's been out there playing in mud and shit," he said, laughing.

"I was at work," I said. "I don't know nothing about this."

"Yeah, right," the other officer said. "Shut up."

I was silent for a while. Then I said, "My cousin works over here. Officer Drink."

"I know him," the second officer said. "As a matter of fact, he's here right now."

I tried not to sound too hopeful. "Could you go get him?" I asked.

"Yeah, I'll get him." Finally, someone was giving me a break.

I told my cousin the whole story and afterward, he said, "I'll take care of it." He returned with the sergeant. They spoke for a couple minutes, then the sergeant said, "Okay, don't worry about it. Since he's your cousin, I'll take care of it." I knew we were getting out of there.

Two hours passed. Then three. I never saw either one again. Not only was the sergeant lying, but my own first cousin was going to believe him over me. My hopes were crushed.

We were taken upstairs to the detectives, who also tried to get us to say we did it. They told us we were going to be charged with aggravated assault and armed robbery, then they added, "If he dies, we're going to upgrade the charge to murder."

My heart was thumping, but all I said was, "I just got off work. I didn't do nothing."

The dicks typed up a statement and told us to sign it. It was our supposed confession. "I ain't signing nothin'," I told them.

I felt all the hatred for that police uniform rush back in. I thought about the day when the traffic cop slapped me for nothing. Here it was twelve years later, and the police had me charged and handcuffed, again for something I didn't do. The same thing was happening, only this time my life was at stake.

Once again, I didn't relate my arrest to being black. To me, it was about the police being blue and thinking that as the law, they were above it, that they could do whatever they wanted, whichever way they wanted, and there was little I or anyone could do about it. It all seemed so unfair. I felt totally helpless.

Looking around the station, I figured it was better to just keep quiet. People were talking continuously. The officers were constantly shouting: "Shut up." "Sit down." "Shut the fuck up." "Sit your ass down." The police were bringing in people screaming and crying. Some were bleeding. Watching this messed-up scene, I told myself, *If I say too much, they'll think I'm being a smartass. And then they might hit me.* I would answer their questions but I wasn't about to argue with them. I knew not to pour gasoline on fire. I wasn't going to raise my voice. I wasn't going to scream. I wasn't going to cry. I would show no emotion.

My opportunity to speak would come later, in court, where I could tell my side of the story. On the way to our arraignment the next day, a sheriff's deputy told John and me what to do once we got inside the courtroom: Keep our hands behind our backs, stand in front of the judge, and look straight ahead. The first time our names were called, we were told the charges: armed robbery and aggravated assault. Then the judge asked me if I had a lawyer. I told him no.

"No, *Your Honor,*" the deputy added.

I didn't care what I said anymore. I was pissed off. Here I was, standing in front of the judge, but I still couldn't tell my side of the story. The deputy led us back to a holding cell, where we waited to meet with the public defender.

A few hours later, we returned to the courtroom. This time, the state's attorney gave a rundown of the incident we were accused of. "They're here for armed robbery. . . . It occurred on the El. . . . The defendant cut the victim across the leg."

I sat there denying every word in my head. I knew enough not to say anything then, but I was still hoping I'd have a chance later to say, "No, Your Honor, what happened was . . ." It never came. The whole courtroom scene was all lawyers versus lawyers.

"Your Honor," the state's attorney said, slicing into my thoughts, "we recommend bond be set at $6,500."

I could have passed out. To walk, I would need $6,500! I knew my parents didn't have that kind of money. I turned to the public defender, who finally spoke up for me.

"Your honor, my client here goes to Catholic school, has never been arrested, has never been in trouble before in his life. He works with his father doing construction work." Here was my chance.

The judged slammed down his gavel. "Bail stands at $6,500."

I couldn't hold my emotions back anymore. A few tears started to fall. I turned around and saw my parents and Rena, who must have gotten word of my arrest, sitting in the courtroom. My mother was hugging my father. Rena gave me a look that said, "There's nothing we can do."

As John and I were escorted back to the holding pen, I thought, *This will be the last time I'll see my family for a long time.* My next court date was set for a month later, and I knew there was no way they could get me out of jail before then. I was headed to the County.

Cook County Jail was a whole other world. As soon as our bus pulled up, the guards began shouting. "Yeah, motherfucker, y'all are in my backyard now," one of them said. "Get your asses off this bus." When I got off the bus, all I could see around me was steel and concrete and barbed wire. I was totally isolated from the rest of the world—and, for that matter, from reality. Reality was outside.

The guards were barking orders, ushering us from one station to another. First station they took me to, I had to strip down to my underwear while they searched me. Then I stepped over to a window, where I was handed two sheets, a toothbrush, and a tube of toothpaste that I was expected to make last for my entire stay.

At another station, about twenty of us stood in a row, buck naked, in front of a nurse and doctor who were checking us for venereal disease. Without saying a word, the doctor grabbed my penis, then took a long cotton swab and—shwoop—pushed it down the head. Pain shot through my body. I wanted to scream, but there was no way I was going to in front of all those men and the nurse. Nobody made so much as a peep.

We then moved to a long hallway, where the guards searched us again before sending us to the tiers and our cells. "Lift your left foot; wiggle your toes," they ordered. "Lift your right foot; wiggle your toes. Now wiggle your fingers; raise your arms."

They were making sure we didn't have anything taped to the soles of our feet or underneath our arms. "Pull up your sack." We lifted up our testicles. "Stretch them." Finally they said, "Now turn around, bend over, and spread your cheeks." Imagine twenty naked men standing in a line, bent over, their hands spreading their asses for all the guards to see. As the guards walked from one end of the line, inspecting one ass at a time, they talked about each of us the whole way. "Yeah, look at him." "He's got a real big ass." "He's probably been fucked up his ass."

They took their time telling us to straighten up. I was way at the other end of the line, bent over but with my hands at my side. I wasn't about to spread my cheeks yet. Just as I was saying to myself how totally humiliating this was, a lieutenant shouted from the hallway, "Hey, get these naked asses in some clothes. It's almost time for dinner." Thank God.

It was almost five o'clock. Nearly twenty-four hours had passed since my ordeal began. We hustled into our clothes, since the County didn't have uniforms back then, and were taken to the tiers.

"Fresh meat, fresh meat," we heard the inmates shouting almost as soon as we walked into the section assigned for sixteen- and seventeen-year-olds. There were five of us who walked in that day, including this one dude named Michael Jackson. He was a short, light-skinned brother who was acting tough.

"I know I'm in here," he said. "Don't even fuck with me. Don't even talk shit."

That was a mistake. The second day, five or six boys grabbed him while he was taking a shower. They were fingering his behind, pulling on his penis, trying to stick their penises in his mouth. He tried to fight them off, but it was no use.

The tier was like one big dormitory hallway. It had twenty cells for two people each, showers, toilets, and a dayroom with a television. There was a small room with a mesh screen where we could talk to our lawyers. But there were no walls anywhere. The bathrooms and the showers were wide open for the guards and everybody else to see you. The cells had steel doors facing the inside of the tier and bars on the other side where the guards could watch us from a catwalk. The guards never entered unless they were coming to kick some ass.

Our tier was overcrowded, mostly with brothers. When John,

who had been with me since our arrest, and I were assigned to a cell, we didn't even have a mattress. I couldn't see sleeping on that cold floor with all the mice running around, so we made our bed on a picnic table in the dayroom.

Our first day there, the lieutenant on duty, a guy named Porch, noticed that John and I had never been in trouble before. We told him our whole story, and he took a liking to us almost as soon as we started talking. "If anybody tries to mess with you, let me know," he told us. "I'll take care of them. And don't let nobody take your manhood away while you're in here." Finally, a friend. But I knew Lieutenant Porch would only be there eight hours out of the day. The other sixteen would be hell.

I sat up that first night in the County. I couldn't believe I was in this mess. I was hungry and I wanted to talk to my family. Staying out in the dayroom made it a little easier. At least I wasn't in a cell behind that steel door. Then I really would have felt trapped. I was trying to keep my mind strong and not cave in to all the emotions I felt. I thought about how I would get out of there soon. I planned the next day in my head: "Okay, I'm not going to be around that group. I'm going to avoid this area." There was no way I was taking a shower. I wasn't about to make myself vulnerable the way Michael Jackson had. I also wasn't planning to hang out. John and I decided to stay mostly to ourselves. Surprisingly, nobody bothered us. Maybe it was because we were so quiet and stuck together. Plus, now we were cool with Lieutenant Porch.

My second day in the County, Rena and the public defender came to visit me. They were trying to get the bond lowered by Friday so I wouldn't have to spend the weekend in jail. Then, Rena told me something that rocked my world. Two guys my older brothers knew had confessed to doing the robbery on the El and turned themselves in to the police. But when they admitted to stabbing the man on the El, the sergeant had turned them away. He'd insisted that he "had his two." He didn't even arrest them. Suddenly, I was filled with rage. If I had seen the sergeant at that moment, I probably would have committed murder.

One morning, a guard called out my name. "The chaplain wants to see you," he said.

My heart began to race and my palms got sweaty. All I could think was, *The victim died.* I followed the guard down a long walkway to the chaplain's office, thinking, *Prison forever. I'm going to be here forever.*

People get their calling in life in different ways. Mine came on the way to the chaplain's office when a thought suddenly popped into my head: *If I ever get out of here, I'm definitely becoming a police officer. I'm going to stop this madness from being perpetrated on somebody else. And at the very least, it will never happen to me again.* The dream I had as a child now seemed real. My fear and anger were turning into determination.

"Relax, relax," the chaplain said when I sat down across from him.

He wore a priest's black robe and white collar, his hair was white, and he looked to be at least sixty. Sitting in his office, I felt almost normal. His room was the closest thing to the outside world. He had pictures on his desk, a couch, wood paneling on the walls. I knew I was still in jail, but at least I was getting a little taste of reality. There were no bars, no guards, just him and me. He told me that my principal, Brother Johnson, was a friend of his. Apparently my mom had asked Brother Johnson to call him. I felt a huge weight lift from my shoulders.

"You can come to school up here, and you won't have to stay around all that nonsense," the chaplain explained. "You will have to read and do some work. You can't just sit in your chair or fall asleep. But at least this way you can stay out of trouble."

"Fantastic," I said.

I started that day, and the next day John was able to come too. We read books and magazines and newspapers and took little tests to keep our skills sharp. It made passing the time a whole lot easier.

One afternoon, about a month later, I was sitting in the dayroom when a guard called out my name. "Get your stuff, Holcomb," he said. "You got bonded out."

I knew my parents had been working hard to bail me out, and it was just a matter of time. So I never lost hope. But it actually took an act of God—or at least one of God's helpers—to get me out.

The chaplain and Brother Johnson had gone to the judge to convince him I was a good kid. The judge had finally agreed and reduced my bond to $5,000. My sister, who was working and had saved up her money, had put up the required 10 percent—$500—so I could walk. Just like before, the chaplain had come through for me.

I ran through the tier to tell John. He gave me a look as if his last friend in the world had died. With his entire family in Mississippi for the summer, I really was all he had. Fighting back tears, he said, "Hey, man, don't forget me." He didn't get out of jail until the end of that summer, when his parents returned.

There were no celebrations when I got home, though everyone was glad to see me. Nobody asked what I had been through, either, and I didn't volunteer to tell them. All Daddy said was, "I hope you learned your lesson. You can't be nosy." I certainly didn't hang out for a long time after that.

During my senior year, I went back and forth to court five or six times. Each time, the victim never showed up. Finally, when I was halfway through the school year, the judge threw out the case. But it didn't end there for me.

Though I was able to pay a lawyer $90 to close my arrest record to the public, nothing can wipe away the memory of what happened. It's something I will carry with me always. There are a lot of young brothers who get locked up, either rightly or wrongly, and come out saying, "Damn, I'm glad I'm out." They try to forget the whole experience or they become what the system has made them out to be: criminals. I decided I was going to learn from this and turn this negative into a positive. I had my mind set on becoming a police officer. Knowing that as an African-American man I would always be a target of the police made me even more resolved to become one of them. This unjust treatment had to stop.

First, I was going to college. About five schools were talking to me about basketball scholarships and I wound up at the University of Illinois at Chicago. But basketball was out: The coach didn't let freshmen or sophomores play. I left college after two years to take a good-paying job servicing buses for the Chicago Transit Authority. But I was still fixed on becoming a police officer. When I took the police test later that same year, Jane Byrne was mayor, and her administration had all these strict requirements designed to keep blacks off the job. Even though I scored real high, all the tests were later thrown out because they were said to be discriminatory against blacks. My next shot was when Harold Washington became the first black mayor. I passed the test and a year later, in 1986, I was invited to attend the Police Academy.

The day before I entered the Academy, my mother's lungs collapsed after years of smoking, and she went into a coma. When she came out of it five months later, she had no idea who I or who any of my brothers and sisters were. She was stuck in her childhood for the last three years of her life. I couldn't bear to see her that way. Even talking to her on the telephone and having her ask every time, "Who are you?" would make me break down. Knowing she'd always wanted me to finish school and become either a doctor or lawyer, I didn't have the heart to tell her I was a police officer.

My father was skeptical of my decision at first, but when he actually saw me in my uniform, I could tell he was proud. He invited me for the first time to sit with his friends and play cards. I knew then I had become a man in his eyes. The entire game, he asked me questions about being a police officer. Here I was actually having a conversation with my father.

Six years after Mom's death, Daddy died from lung cancer, too.

The biggest regret I have about coming from a big family is how great the loss feels after each death. We were closer than most families because our father made us stick together in everything. My brothers and sisters became my best friends. Now, I almost hate to think about all the good times we had together. Just before Daddy passed, Monroe died from cirrhosis of the liver. He was the only brother who still worked with Daddy every day. Maybe that's how he picked up our father's drinking habit, and lost his own family because of it. In 1996, my younger brother Daryl passed away from AIDS after a long addiction to heroin, and now Greg is sick from the same thing. I'm tired of seeing all this death. It's taken me from being the fourth youngest boy to the next to the oldest.

What saved me from going the same route as my brothers was my dream of becoming a police officer. I skipped a lot of hanging out, drinking, and getting high to get here. Now my role in the family has become clear to me. I'm not the black sheep I always thought I was; I am a father and a police officer. And though it came late, I finally got praise from my father for who I am.

Without him and the rest of my family, I wouldn't be where I am today. They were the first to give me hope that I could achieve and become whoever I wanted to be. But there were other forces at work, too. I was a good Catholic-school boy from a strong, caring family, yet my only contacts with the police before I became an officer were always negative. If it hadn't been for the injustices I experienced at the hands of the police, I may not have become a police officer.

I had a lot of positives guiding me, too. In life, you run across many people whom you often overlook or take for granted. Some of them are even disguised as your adversaries, but in the end, they may actually help you. I wasn't fond of Catholic school, but my principal came through for me when I was in jail. Without him, the chaplain might never have reached out. Lieutenant Porch, who was part of that unjust system, went out of his way to be nice and make my stay easier. To me, they were rays of hope in a potentially hopeless situation.

Now, as a police officer, I like to think I provide people with that same hope—a torch that gets passed along, from one generation to another.

# Three:
# Where
# We're Going

# 6: Lead
# by Example

*Ain't it a shame, caught up in a gang game.*
*Now your trial date is set.*
*You break out in a cold sweat, hoping and praying,*
  *saying what*
*I do to get in the situation.*
*Well, just think back, and check out how you really act.*
*First you slang, then you bang.*
*Now the police and judge change everything.*
—FROM "AIN'T IT A SHAME" BY THE SLICK BOYS

Among the three of us, Randy, James, and I have been in the projects, the gangs, and the prison system. We've been everywhere the kids we pick up have been, and many of our experiences are almost—but not quite—identical. Some small twist of fate, one moment of clarity, one helping hand gave each of us the hope, ambition, and self-respect that ultimately led us to the police force rather than to jail. When we look back, it seems that all along we were somehow being prepared for the work we're doing now.

A couple of years ago, neighborhood activist Marian Stamps said to us, "God sent y'all." Obviously not everyone felt that way.

Around the same time, a song by the rap group N.W.A. called "Fuck the Police" became Cabrini-Green's anthem. We heard the song everywhere we went. People would blast it on their car stereos when we drove by, and make a point to have it playing when we entered their building. It was as if the residents were saying to each other, "Watch out, 21 and Eddie Murphy are here."

We didn't enjoy hearing "Fuck the Police" all night for a very significant reason. Rap is like CNN for these kids—it's how they get their information about the world. The music can really affect how they think and what they do. We worried that kids might adopt the anti-police attitude the song promoted. One night, James tried talking about this song to a few twelve- and thirteen-year-old boys who were standing around, listening to it. The kids just laughed. "Ah, y'all is just jealous cuz y'all can't rap," one of them teased. James, unable to resist a challenge, shot back, "Anybody can rap. We can do anything we put our minds to. So can you." The next thing I knew, he had talked us—me *and* the kids—into a competition to come up with the best rap song.

Neither James nor I had ever rapped in our lives. But if we were going to prove our point to the kids, we had to do it right. We asked Randy to join us, and formed the Slick Boys, using the slang name for undercover cops. We called on all of our connections: A former gang member named Lottie helped us write three rap songs and a musician friend of James's came up with some original music. Then we put everything together at a studio.

Three weeks after making our bet, we went back to the boys in Cabrini ready to go. They barely had half a rap finished. "Stand back," James said, slipping our tape into his car stereo. The bass was pounding, and the boys broke into the "homeboy nod," bobbing their heads to the beat. "Hey, that's on," one of them said. "Where did you get that track?" Before we knew it, a crowd had formed around us. "Is that really y'all?" someone wanted to know. Now that we had our audience, we started to rap.

At that moment, we crossed over. We were no longer police officers, or supercops, or even 21, Eddie Murphy, or Faheem. We were brothers. As Randy says, the music placed us in *their* world. We realized that here was a way we could touch even more young lives. Pat Hill, the president of the Afro-American Patrolmen's League, recognized it, too. She had a role-model program called We Care that sent black professionals to talk to elementary school students. She invited us to perform our rap songs in the classroom and say a few words to the kids. At first I said no, figuring that since most of the kids were real rap fans, they wouldn't be too impressed—especially once they found out we were cops. But Pat disagreed: "No, it's much bigger than that. It's much bigger than the rap."

She was right, of course, though that didn't make our first performance any easier. A month later, we stood in front of an auditorium full of children, more frightened than if we had just walked into gang war crossfire. We performed with just our portable stereo and the school's microphone and the kids went wild, clapping and dancing in their seats. We visited more than twenty schools that year, and every time, the students cheered.

The whole time we'd had the answers. We'd been saying the problem is that there are no role models in this community—and there we were! With kids asking, "So where did you guys grow up?" Suddenly, we realized, hey, we grew up here. Right here. We figured that not only did we grow up here, we could tell them *how* to grow up here. We could tell them everything that we did and make it like a map. And if they follow it, it doesn't mean they're going to the be president of the United States, but they'll be alive. Just being alive is all right.

It wasn't that we were telling them anything new or different. But it wasn't Mom or Dad preaching to them. We looked like them: three guys with a rap beat on, wearing sunglasses and tank-top T-shirts. They were thinking, "Kids are dying from drug overdoses, drunk driving, gangs. We don't want to die. Tell us how not to die." So we would tell them the truth in a way that's common sense. In a slick way. In a way that is necessary.

In the fall of 1992, the media discovered us. The attention led to more invitations from schools and civic groups throughout the city. The next spring, we took our act on the road, going to other areas that shared Cabrini's problems. Now, we've been to over twenty-five states, including Arkansas, Colorado, Missouri, and Texas, and to a few other countries, including Germany, Cuba, and Nigeria. We've performed at juvenile detention centers, drug rehabilitation clinics, Native American reservations, colleges, police departments, prisons—any place our message might have an impact.

Our act is more polished now—we have professional sound equipment and dancers—but the music will always be secondary to the message. We use rap to grab kids' attention. Rap music is a huge part of life in the projects—for kids everywhere, in fact. In many ways, it serves as young peoples' education. Yet, so much of the rap that's out there sends negative messages, encouraging violence, lack of respect for women and for self, gang activity, and killing.

We use the power of rap to educate. We make sure our music has more to offer than entertainment, whether it's a lesson about making good choices or assuming responsibility, or a view of the world outside the projects. All of our songs are meant to communicate something of value to these kids.

But it's what we tell kids after a performance that sticks with them most. Those talks are what makes us more than cops who happen to rap. We're real people who have been through what *they're* going through—and have gotten out.

When we first started going to schools, we kept our speeches short and simple: Stay away from gangs and drugs, and stay in school. Then we slowly let more of our personal lives slip into our talks. The more we shared our experiences from childhood, the more kids responded. The stories helped them understand and relate to us. These children are hungry for direction and role models in their lives. Many of their fathers, mothers, sisters, and brothers are in gangs, on drugs, in jail, or dead. Because of where we come from, young people see themselves in us. When we talk about our pasts, they see we faced the same obstacles they do. Hearing how we overcame those obstacles gives them hope.

In many ways, forming the Slick Boys was a natural progression in our policing strategy. We always knew that locking people up accomplished very little and, in fact, was often counterproductive. And since we talked mainly with the guys we arrested, our chances of having an impact on the larger community were limited. So, we started chasing bad guys less, and talking to good kids more. If we could reach people at a younger age—*before* they got into trouble—maybe we could prevent them from ever committing a crime.

We also knew that to avoid becoming jaded by our work in the inner city, we would have to be more creative with our policing. If all you're doing is locking people up every day, it's easy to start feeling helpless, to think, *They're just going to kill each other anyway, so what good am I doing?* We were becoming so inured to the horrors in the projects that after a year, we were no longer shocked to hear that a little kid was killed in gang crossfire. In some ways, that callousness made facing our jobs on a daily basis easier, but that kind of apathy helps no one. To lift ourselves and the community up, we needed to stay fresh and involved.

Performing as the Slick Boys helped us to do that. It gave us a new way to interact with the kids who needed us most, and those interactions were constant reminders that each of them was a unique and special case. It also expanded the number of communities we could reach.

We can walk into any place in the country with fifty to a hundred Disciples and Vice Lords or Bloods and Crips and get treated with respect, not because we are the police, but because we come to them as fellow human beings.

When I lectured recently at Harvard about our work with gangs, a professor asked me why kids in Boston respond to me as if I grew up on the same streets they did. "It's because I'm talking about their lives," I told him. Our experiences transcend generational as well as geographical lines.

When we first became the Slick Boys, the police department didn't want any part of us. The word "rap" made most officers think of gangbangers and drive-by shootings. In Chicago, as in a lot of other cities, the guys running the department were in many ways detached from what was happening on the streets. They were used to collecting data on how many tickets, arrests, or busts were made. We were talking music and education—not exactly things they could get hard data on. Only a few officers had begun to think about more creative policing strategies, so even if some people in the department knew that what we were doing made sense, they couldn't justify it to the politicians who ran the show—and who needed that hard data to keep them in office.

We were even told that the department already had a crime prevention program: Officer Friendly, an officer who tells elementary school kids to stay away from drugs, avoid talking to strangers, and not touch matches. He might even bring along McGruff, the crime dog, who is really an officer dressed in a furry costume. This program is great for younger age groups, but most kids living in the projects grow up so fast that by the third grade, they're too jaded to be moved by such simple advice and crime-fighting canines. After third grade, the program's effectiveness starts to fall off. But young people still need some kind of positive contact with the police. Their next encounter with a cop shouldn't be when they're getting arrested.

Until we could convince the police department that what we were doing was useful, we had to keep all of our Slick Boys activities separate from our official job. By day, we were the Slick Boys, undercover cops who rap. By night, we were Eric, James, and Randy, cops policing the projects. We'd work our regular 6 P.M. to 2 A.M. shift, go home, catch a few hours of sleep, and perform at a school later that morning. We'd use our weekends and vacations to take our message outside of Chicago.

Some of our fellow officers in the public housing division were a little suspicious of the good rapport we had with the residents. They couldn't figure out how the three of us, who worked the fewest number of hours per week, could have a better relationship with the residents *and* get more police work done. I think some officers were even jealous because we were enjoying our jobs so much.

Becoming the Slick Boys made our jobs easier. But that was because we had invested so much time already. We had been putting our hearts and souls into these communities for a long time, and the people living there knew it. After the truce in Cabrini, we could barely go one block in the patrol car without someone flagging us down to say hello. Gang leaders, who ordinarily would give a violation to anyone who talked to the police, always made exceptions in our case—they would even talk to us themselves. Aspiring rappers would round us up to hear their latest creations. We'd hoop in the park with the fellas, or just hang out on the building stoop and talk. We were invited to so many barbecues, birthday parties, and Bulls' games, we had to establish a "no-eating-on-the-job" policy, to keep ourselves focused.

Having such a good relationship with these neighborhoods changed the way we worked. In the Village, all we had to do was park the patrol car and the residents would tell us what to do. The older ladies would inform us, "They're selling drugs over there," or "They're putting guns in those Dumpsters." The gang members would find us and say, "They're getting ready to shoot out of that apartment."

At Cabrini, we were like Sheriff Taylor and Barney from the old *Andy Griffith Show*. Some guys would never think of turning themselves in to anyone but us. In the summer of 1996, a Vice Lord named Andrew came up to our car and told us he wanted to turn himself in for stealing a drug addict's money. We told Andrew to sit tight until we could go over to the district police station and locate the report on the robbery. While we searched for the report for the next several days, the district police, who actually had the report with them, came looking for Andrew. Every time they got close, he would run and hide in the building. Then, he'd hit us on our pagers. "I'm ready to turn myself in," he would say. "Andrew, we still haven't found the report." He did this four or five times, including the day we were off, until the addict decided to drop the case.

The biggest supporters of the Slick Boys have always been the people in the projects. They understand that we're about more than just the rap. They see us trying to bring something positive to the community and they believe in what we're doing. Older gang members come up to us with a son or younger brother, saying things like, "I want you to talk some sense into him. I don't want him to be like me." Or they send us letters from the penitentiary, giving us permission to whip their sons' butts when they get out of line. They believe we can set examples for the children.

What convinced our commander that we were for real was an incident in the spring of 1993, not long after the truce between the gangs in Cabrini. A Gangster Disciple accused a Vice Lord of talking to his girlfriend. Things escalated quickly, and the Disciple pulled a gun on him. In defense, the Vice Lord grabbed a twelve-year-old boy and used him as a human shield. The Disciple shot and killed both of them. Two more young lives wasted in a split second of insanity.

At about seven the next morning, I got a call from the mayor's press coordinator. She wanted the Slick Boys to go over to Cabrini right away, so we could diffuse any tensions. Still half-asleep after finishing my shift just hours earlier, I hung up the phone thinking, *This isn't really happening.* But it was.

When we got to Cabrini, everyone we knew was there: our former commander Robert Guthrie, our friend and supporter Marian Stamps, and Wallace "Gator" Bradley, the spokesperson for the Disciples. We walked over to the 500 W. Oak building, where most of the Vice Lords stay, grabbed the leaders, and made them meet with the Gangster Disciple bosses. Then we stood back. "Let them talk," I told the commander when he protested.

After about ten minutes, the guys parted and walked over to us. "It's straight," they said. The Disciples had agreed to pay for the funerals of the two young men who were killed and to "take care" of the guy who'd shot them. The shooter was subsequently arrested and given a life sentence. And when he arrived in jail, he apparently caught hell from his own gang. Both the gang and the judicial system were sending him a message: Such actions would no longer be tolerated in the community.

If the two gangs had not communicated, this event could have led to further fighting and an end to the truce. What we had done was act as a bridge between the two groups. Both gangs knew who we were and what we stood for, and our presence enabled them to come to a peaceful conclusion on their own. But ultimately, they took responsibility for holding together their community, which is what we wanted all along when we sat them down the first time to hammer out a truce. Though we had taken very little action, the result was enough to convince Commander Guthrie to ask us to bring the Slick Boys program to the Robert Taylor project.

The moment we got there, we knew it wasn't going to happen as quickly and easily as the commander had hoped. We didn't know any of the residents, and the smallest building was nineteen stories. It was like starting out in Cabrini all over again.

We decided to begin with the building where the police substation was housed. Even there, we saw guys running to shoot at some guys from another building. Whenever we walked into a building, the gang members would scatter. Then, one day, one of them stopped and asked, "Hey, aren't you the Slick Boys?" When he approached us, his buddies followed, and before we knew it, a dialogue had opened up between us and the Taylor residents.

That summer of 1993, we started a baseball league featuring Taylor and the other South Side housing development teams. We helped the Gangster Disciples and the Cobra Stones at Dearborn Homes set up a truce that's been going strong for two years now.

It was Commander Guthrie's idea for us to put on our Slick Boys T-shirts and ride bicycles through the projects. He wanted us to have closer contact with the residents. That didn't last long—we couldn't even bike a few yards without people stopping us. Everybody wanted a Slick Boys button or a T-shirt or an autograph. We would look behind us and see about twenty kids on their bikes, following us. We even let some of the kids who didn't have bikes ride ours while we walked through Taylor or Stateway Gardens or Lathrop Homes, just meeting and talking to people.

What we were doing was really nothing new. We were just like the beat cops of the 1950s, who patrolled a neighborhood on foot and knew everyone who lived there. When cities all over America put cops in patrol cars, they removed this very special interaction between people and police. Fortunately, the concept of community policing has been revived in the nineties. We've brought our own twist to the job: We wear sunglasses, combat boots, and baggy jeans, and we rap. There are other officers out there who, for years, have been going beyond the call of duty. Now, with community policing once again the standard strategy in Chicago and other U.S. cities, all officers should have a better relationship with the communities in which they work.

Community policing is nothing more than the neighborhood and the police working together. With our department's program, the Chicago Alternative Policing Strategy, we can call on the city's resources to address any problem in the neighborhood, whether it's getting graffiti removed, an abandoned car towed, a streetlight fixed, or new plumbing installed for a public housing resident. This approach makes the best use of police officers who are in the neighborhood every day. It also forces officers to leave their patrol cars, get to know the folks in the neighborhood, and once again put on a human face. It also empowers the people who live in those neighborhoods by reminding them that we work for them. Community policing reconnects police officers to their mission to "Serve and Protect." We are, after all, public *servants*. We believe community policing has the potential to be the best thing that ever happened to law enforcement in our country.

After Commander Guthrie retired, Michael Tolliver took over. He's been a big supporter of community policing—and the Slick Boys—from the start. "We've used the Slick Boys as peacekeepers," Tolliver explains. "Whenever we get wind of a problem between gangs, we send Eric, Randy, and James to talk to both of the leaders. There is a mutual respect between them and the community, as even the troublemakers recognize and admire them. But they are still no-nonsense police officers."

It was Commander Tolliver's idea to set up a learning center in Robert Taylor. Tolliver believes in giving people every opportunity to better themselves. He got several dozen computers donated and an instructor to come teach free GED classes. We encourage people to come to the center. We also donated enough exercise equipment to start a weight room there. Our idea is that once people start working on their bodies, it's just a short step to working on their minds. It's easier as an officer to just do your job on the street—in the projects, that's challenging enough—but it's much tougher to deal with people's hearts and minds.

When black children turn twelve or thirteen, many parents sit them down for "the talk." This talk is not about sex; it's about how to handle themselves when they're confronted by the police: "When the police call you nigger, don't say anything to them. You just say, 'Yes, sir,' no matter what they do." My mama gave me that talk, and I know many mothers who are still giving it today. But I refuse to give that talk to my daughter.

As the Slick Boys, we strive to be examples of good police officers, whether it's by doing our job well on the streets or by showing the men and women we work with that police brutality, bias, and dishonesty will not be tolerated. A lot of problems—in the force *and* on the streets—would be eliminated if officers would stop averting their eyes when they see a fellow officer doing something to someone they would not want done to their own families. We've followed that guideline since we left the Academy and we think police officers all over the country need to follow it, too.

Though the vast majority of police officers are good-hearted, upstanding citizens, some lose perspective in the course of doing their job. People in the neighborhoods are always telling us about how a cop "put something on them"—planted drugs in their homes or in their clothing. It's probably true. Unfortunately, some cops resort to this when they know someone's selling but they can't catch the dealer in the act. Others don't report all the drugs and money they confiscate when they *do* catch someone. Vance "Vino" Simmons was once the victim of this kind of unethical policing. "This cop and about seven or eight of his buddies searched my house and saw I had a floor safe," Vino says. "When I asked them if they had a search warrant, the cop put a gun to my head and cocked it. 'I don't need a search warrant. Open up the safe.' They took about $15,000 that I had saved up, then left."

This uniform we wear is not a Superman suit. When we are deceitful, our actions will eventually catch up with us. Rumor has it that one officer who worked in Cabrini used to take people's dope but not arrest them. One day, the Cobra Stones mixed up a deadly bag of stuff, knowing the officer would take it. He did, and later died.

We earned the respect of the community by never straying from our rule: If we catch you doing wrong, we lock you up. Initially, the gangs tested us. They offered us bribes. Our standard reply was we will never do anything to hurt the community or embarrass our families. After a while, the gang members stopped offering us money; instead, they started filing false complaints about us. If they couldn't kill us or buy us off, maybe they could get us transferred. Finally, they had to accept that we weren't going anywhere, though they didn't quite believe it. They used to ask, "Y'all really believe in this shit, don't you?" One guy, Dupree, who we've seen go from gangbanger to barbershop owner, describes us as "good guys." Dupree says, "Some police don't think of you as people—they think of you as inmates. The project's like a penitentiary to them. But these Slick Boys come to you with respect. They don't want to see you in trouble, because they seen you grow up. They trying to step positive, help us out, get us off the streets."

It takes special police officers to work in poor inner-city neighborhoods. For so long, those areas have received inferior service or none at all. We need officers, both black and white, who can bring understanding and compassion to their jobs. Just using words like "sir" or "ma'am"—that is, showing some respect to the residents— would go a long way toward alleviating problems and tensions. Fortunately, with mandatory cultural awareness classes for new recruits and community policing strategies in place, we are seeing more officers who are not only better educated but more sensitive to citizens' needs.

The most dangerous aspect of being a police officer is the potential for abuse of the power we're given. For some, such power is too much to handle. Some officers confuse this power with personal power. That's what leads to incidents like the infamous Rodney King beating, which, in 1992, sparked violent riots against the police in the Los Angeles area. What each of us has to understand is that *real* power comes from being a good person.

And we are always being presented with opportunities to be good people. As the Slick Boys, we won't tell children—or adults, for that matter—to do something. Instead, we'll try to *show* them.

# 7: Don't Play to the Stereotypes

*If people stereotype you, that's limiting. But if you become a stereotype, it can cripple you and destroy any chance you may have for success.*

Gangster. Dope dealer. Mugger. These are the stereotypes of young black men that many Americans subscribe to. They are infuriating, but what makes us even madder is how often young brothers choose to assume these roles. It's almost as if the stereotypes become self-fulfilling prophecies. "If this is how they see us," they seem to tell themselves, "then this is how we'll be." Frank McFadden, who grew up in Cabrini, explains how easy it is to give in to such stereotypes:

> I joined the Disciples the summer after I graduated. I was seventeen years old and already had my first child. Wendy's was paying only $4.15 an hour—it wasn't what my friends who were gangsters were making. When I joined, my life took a turn for the better on the street side. The girls I had wanted to go with were all impressed with the gangsters. If you didn't have long hair and weren't known as a gangbanger, you couldn't have the girl of your choice. Suddenly the girls were like, "Who's that?"

I really wasn't into selling drugs all that hard. I made only about $8,000 in six months. Frankly, I was afraid of losing my life. Once, a guy fired at me as I was coming out of a building—the bullet shot right by my face. And there was the guilt factor. When I started going to Truman College, all these older folks would say, "I'm so proud of you. You didn't go the way of those other knuckleheads." That used to hit me in the heart, because they wanted me to be the savior, the one to inspire other kids to believe that they could make it too. My mom, who was doing everything in her power to see me make it, would hear rumors about me being in a gang. But she always gave me the benefit of the doubt. Eddie Murphy, who also had his suspicions, would tell me I needed to get my music together—I'd wanted to be a rapper since I was in seventh grade. Everything I was saying to them was a lie, and it was starting to bug me.

Finally, I told the guys in the gang I didn't want this no more. Luckily, there was so much changing of the guard and so many wars, they couldn't worry about me. Recently, I was walking through Cabrini with a girl I was dating and her friend, and this cop threw me up against the car. He started digging in my pants, which is degrading, then said, "Let me see some ID." He looked in my wallet and found my college ID. "You go to Truman?" he asked. I told him "Yeah." Then he said, "Well, keep up the good work and we won't have to bother you anymore." I get a lot of that stereotype stuff. It's cool because now I'm proving everyone wrong—I have a good-paying, full-time job, and I'm supporting my daughter. But it's sad that I have to prove myself again and again.

Fortunately, Frank got past the stereotypes before he got hurt. But too often, our young black men are killing each other as they play out these stereotypes. And they are being killed—and incarcerated—by a society that is more and more threatened by such stereotypes. The Mob Action Law (which says you can be arrested just for hanging out with your buddies), the three-strikes-and-you're-out laws, and various drug laws target inner-city populations. The proof is that black men are going to prison in record numbers and a disproportionate number of African Americans are in the prison population. Even more disturbing, the police can actually profit from crime, especially in communities such as the projects.

James explains that he can lock up ten different people for selling ten different bags of dope, get ten different court dates, and get paid overtime ten times for going to court. Police officers are policing poor communities for dollars. There are rules for poor folks and rules for everybody else. The judge gives the white boy a verbal warning and the brother a trial date. Crime pays everybody but the person who commits it.

Ironically, the more Americans focus on negative stereotypes of young black men, the more we keep missing the real drug dealers. Most of the guys we deal with on a daily basis are at the bottom of the drug-dealing food chain. Vino claims that often the middleman is "a white guy who sells dope to us and then we turn around and sell it to our brothers and sisters. We distribute it; we don't grow it. If you want to stop drugs, start at the top." The drug business in Cabrini-Green or ABLA is the tip of the iceberg. The big guys—the drug honchos—are in Colombia, Mexico, Vietnam, wherever these drugs are grown and exported to the United States. Equally culpable are the companies in this country that sell a chemical to Colombia that enhances heroin production.

The three of us aren't immune to stereotypes either. Even with our badges and ID, we are often pegged as criminals. Once, we were riding around in plainclothes when we heard a robbery-in-progress call in the upscale Lincoln Park area. Since we were nearby, we responded. We knocked on the door, identified ourselves, and flashed our badges at the peephole. After a while, we heard another call on the car radio for the same address, this time about three suspicious-looking black men. "Damn, that's us," we said. We radioed back to the squad and told them to send some white uniformed officers.

On another occasion, Randy had left his house in his red Jeep Cherokee and was passing through Englewood, a neighborhood with a lot of gang activity, when three undercover police officers pulled him over. Because he'd been stopped before, he knew to get out of the car with his badge in hand and not make any sudden moves. "There's a lot of phony badges and IDs out here," this white cop said to him. Randy answered, "The only thing phony out here is you." Then the guy started asking questions about where Randy worked, how long he'd been on the job, and so on. Finally, Randy said, "Look, I identified myself, now I've got things to do," and left. I wonder how Randy would have been treated if he hadn't had a badge.

What's even more disturbing is that these stereotypes are not only held by white cops, or middle-class suburbanites, but by the people who are being stereotyped. One of our biggest fears as black officers, especially working undercover, is that we'll be mistaken for the bad guys. It's what burns out a lot of blacks on the job. They can't take the pressure of not knowing who's going to shoot them. I used to tell Jimmy, "I wear my vest for the police and carry my gun for the criminals."

The experience that connected us most to other brothers was when we went to the South Side to see some old heads about vandalized police cars. They were playing basketball and invited us to play, so we put our guns and radios in the trunk and joined them on the court. Afterward, we talked to them about being responsible men in the neighborhood and cooperating with the police. As we were talking, about fifteen Chicago Housing Authority police officers surrounded us with their guns drawn and put everybody up against the wall—including us. Any sudden moves and we could have been shot. When we were finally able to identify ourselves, we didn't try to embarrass the other officers for their mistake, although the gang members wanted us to. Instead, they saw that we go through the same crap that they go through. We get put up against the wall just like they do, yet we still believe this society can offer more than the world of gangs and dope.

Stereotypes are demeaning. They demean those who choose to fulfill them and they demean those who subscribe to them. They are also dangerous—they can literally kill. When kids swallow the stereotype that doing and selling drugs is cool, they may pay with their lives. We're also concerned about those who characterize all inner-city youth as gang members and drug dealers. That stereotype kills any understanding of and communication with young people who are desperately in need of help.

As damaging as the stereotypes are, so are the anti-drug clichés: "Just Say No" and "Just Don't Do It" are glib political slogans that do not address the very real pressures and needs that kids feel. Vino Simmons explains that gangs and drugs are "a way of life in the projects. To stand still is to die. That means if you don't have no money, you can't go nowhere. People in the projects want to look good, live in luxury, have something. They don't want to stay down."

Vino thought he was living his dream life when he was dealing drugs. He lived on Argayle Street and paid his monthly $700 rent a year in advance. He drove nice cars—a Chevy Malibu and a Chevy Impala—and his girlfriend had a Park Avenue Buick. "We had jewelry," recalls Vino. "We were going out to dinner, eating filet mignon. I could buy my children whatever they wanted." But, as Vino learned, if you live too high a life, the police know who you are.

Vino went to prison in 1985, but that two and half years turned out to be the best time of his life because he accomplished something: a GED, a chef's license, and an emergency medical technician's license. "I used to think that the police would end up killing me on the streets," Vino says. "But now I choose life. I would never go back to throwing bricks at the penitentiary, or doing dirt for the gangs.

"It *is* hard finding work, though, because nobody wants to hire somebody with my background. I've worked a couple of jobs, but now I'm looking again."

Living in the projects doesn't keep you from wanting the American dream, but it does change how you go about achieving it. Vino went from being governor of the Gangster Disciples and overseeing all the gang members from downtown Chicago to Evanston to being another unemployed man with a drug habit who lives with his girlfriend and their children in Cabrini. Why should his only choices be to end up broke, with a drug habit, or to peddle drugs? Most people who sell drugs in the projects do so because their choices are so limited. Contrary to the stereotype, they don't sell drugs to buy fancy cars or jewelry; they sell drugs to buy Pampers and to pay the rent. Every dealer we've talked to has said as much:

If I had a job, I wouldn't be selling drugs. Even the guys in ABLA, who were raking in the dough, told us the same thing.

In ABLA, dope peddling was run like a real business. Customers came from Cabrini, Wilmette, Schaumburg, even downstate to get "the bomb," the best dope. Maps showing how to get to ABLA were circulated in many of the white suburban schools. Stepping into the Village was like walking into a pharmacy. Every street offered a different drug. Coke was sold on Washburn, heroin on 13th Street, and wickie sticks—joints dipped in PCP—were sold on Hastings. There was even a drive-thru service. Most of the dope spots were open twenty-four hours a day, rain or shine.

You'd be surprised at what *does* shut dealers down. On one occasion, Jimmy and I arrived at the Village to find the players "clean"—all dressed up and free of drugs. "We're closed," one of them explained. "It's a holiday." The holiday was the birthday of one of their leaders, which just happened to coincide with opening night of the new Steven Seagal movie. After that, we knew that whenever a new Seagal or Jean-Claude Van Damme movie opened, the drug business in ABLA closed down for the night.

Too bad it's not so easy to shut down the drug business for good. If it were, the Chicago police would have hired Steven Seagal a long time ago. Unfortunately, Americans keep looking for easy solutions to the country's drug problem. Even the police, overwhelmed by the sheer volume of drugs, can only scratch the surface. Working undercover, Randy, Jimmy, and I have all posed as decoy drug buyers. We would knock on the door of a suspected drug mart. After we bought the dope, we would return the next day with a search warrant and backed up by other cops. We could do this 365 days a year and still be nowhere; as soon as we'd lock up one crew, another would be waiting to take their place.

We discovered that the best way to slow down business in ABLA was to park our car—and sit in it. The dealers knew that as soon as we made a couple of arrests, they could go back to business as usual. Sometimes they would even come over and tell us, "Hey, they're selling drugs down there," just so we'd leave. We didn't always take the bait, though. Often, we'd ask them, "How much money we messing up tonight?" At first they got pissed when we began hanging around, but then they got used to us and opened up. Our jibes became real conversations. We talked to them about school, basketball, life. Over and over, we heard Vino's story: They were trying to take care of themselves and their families, and dealing was their easiest option. Dealing drugs is the one job that's always available in these communities.

The most devastating impact of this scenario is on the kids. If we don't give them choices other than dealing drugs or living in poverty, children start to believe that they are trapped. That's when it's easy for the gangs to move in, for the dope man to get to them. Joining gangs and dealing drugs becomes their only way to get out.

A case in point is Paul. Jimmy and I met him at ABLA's drug drive-thru. We'd been driving by in an unmarked squad car when we spotted him: a little boy holding up a handful of wickie sticks. When we pulled up, he could barely see over the car door, he was so small. Then he realized we were Five-0 and dropped the sticks on the ground and kicked them under the car. "What you got in your hands?" Jimmy said, grabbing him by the jacket, as I went around to pick up the PCP. "Nothing, nothing," he protested. As we were driving to the station, we started talking to him. He told us he was only eleven years old. His mother was dead, his father and his older brother were both in prison for murder. Paul was staying with his grandmother, who was too old to keep an eye on him. He was taking care of himself the only way he knew how. "How much money you make doing this?" we asked him. "On Fridays and Saturdays," he answered, "I make anywhere from $300 to $450 a night."

We could arrest Paul a hundred times and it would not make him change. He would still need to survive somehow. The real problem isn't selling dope; it's that America has given up on some Americans instead of giving them a way to better themselves. People need food, clothing, and shelter to survive, but America doesn't tell you *how* to get those things. Our kids hear, "Make money, make money; fast money is the way."

Some critics of the Cabrini peace treaty say it didn't finish the job because the gangs are still selling drugs. It's true that the gangs are still dealing and sales have probably increased since the shooting stopped. Gang members didn't put down their guns just because the violence was hurting business. They stopped because they got tired. But they did *not* stop needing to eat and feed their families. In projects like ABLA, drug dealing is rarely considered criminal by the residents: It's a community operation. It's also considered better, certainly more honorable, than doing nothing to support your family. Unemployed guys told us they took a $20-an-hour job as a drug lookout to tide them over until they could find a real job. What they really needed were jobs that would pay a decent wage.

Aside from the truce, not much else in Cabrini has changed. There is still a lack of jobs, of job training, and of alcohol and drug rehabilitation programs. We can't just expect people to change without giving them sufficient tools. You have to support them, too, so they can resist the pressure to start using. It's time that we all open our hearts and examine what we're doing to each other. When we do that, it is easy to come up with many, many ways to help. The effort can be as simple as song or as complicated as college. Here is a small sampling of the best America has to offer:

• Zumix is an unusual outreach organization for disadvantaged neighborhood youths in East Boston, Massachusetts. In addition to a drug prevention program, a music mentoring program matches adult musicians with young people and an audio/video/computer training program prepares participants for entry into the work force.

• The Total Experience Gospel Choir, led by volunteer Pat Wright in Seattle, Washington, has helped more than five hundred children in its twenty years. Wright not only provides the kids with a joyful focus for their energy and with increased self-esteem, she also obtains shoes and clothes when necessary. Forty percent of choir members have gone on to earn higher degrees, while all of them have had an opportunity to travel around the country.

• In the Kenilworth projects of Washington, D.C., a single mother named Kimi Gray managed to get off welfare and send all five of her children to college. But she didn't stop there. She helped send *eight hundred* kids in her public housing development to college.

• Former public school teachers Jack Jacqua and Joseph Marshall founded the Omega Boys Club in San Francisco in 1987. Believing that troubled youth were underdeveloped resources, they worked to redirect their lives. They subsequently proved that these young people could turn themselves around when eight of the first fifteen club members attended college. The OBC not only showed them alternatives to crime, but financed their college education and invested in their future.

Here in Chicago, we have found jobs for anywhere from fifty to a hundred men and women in the projects. We'll even give them a job working with the Slick Boys if we can't find them anything else. Jake was one of the guys who worked for us. Like a lot of guys staying in Cabrini, he was homeless—his mom had kicked him out of the house—and unemployed. But, at age twenty-eight, he seemed like a basically responsible, intelligent guy. So I asked him to move in with my mother and keep an eye on her. Then, we employed Jake as the sound man on our videos and helped him get a job clerking in a liquor store in Cabrini. One night, I was watching the TV show *America's Most Wanted* and saw a man who looked a lot like Jake. The report called him Darrell Parker and said he was wanted on federal assault charges. It concluded by saying he was armed and dangerous. I threw on my clothes and rushed over to the liquor store to find Jake. "You're fixing to leave here right now," I said, barely holding back my anger. "You have to turn yourself in." Apologizing profusely, Jake explained to us what had happened. While working at the post office, he had gotten into a fight with another man. He was given probation and regularly reported to his probation officer, until the notices stopped coming. Jake thought he had fulfilled all of his requirements; his probation officer thought he had skipped town.

As much as it hurt us to see Jake go to jail, we knew he had to make things right with the law. He had no other choice but to turn himself in. He spent seven months in prison, and right after he got out, we took him back on the road with us. Our feeling has always been that if you can give people a chance on their own terms, you can find the good in them. Whatever problems arise after that, you can deal with, as long as you feel good about the person. We felt good about Jake from the beginning, and about two months after we took him back, he applied for a job with UPS in Atlanta. He got the job, and now he has his own home.

We also helped one man start up his own business. Andre was twenty years old and heavily involved in a gang when we met him in Robert Taylor a few years ago. But he was begging for a way out. So, we put him to work as a Slick Boys crew member, during which he showed us how diligent and reliable he was. When he decided to open a barbershop on the South Side, we helped him finance it. Now he has three other guys working for him.

Our ultimate goal is to create more centers like the one we helped set up at Robert Taylor. We think they are the solution to a lot of what ails the projects, so we've been applying for grants to fund more of them. We should have another center open soon in Wentworth Gardens on the South Side, and, following on the heels of what we've done, the Chicago Housing Authority has opened a similar center in Cabrini. When people focus their minds on improving themselves, they are less likely to get into trouble or tear apart their community, which means less police work for us.

The money we get from records, performances, and the TV show *New York Undercover,* for which we are consultants, goes right back into the community through a foundation we started in 1993. The Slick Boys Foundation purchases school supplies for elementary school children in public housing, gives scholarships to college-bound graduates, supports a 26-team baseball league for kids and a basketball program for older guys, and funds drug and alcohol treatment for parents. We turned a drug mart at Winthrop and Thorndale Streets into a playground. And we routinely contribute to the families of officers injured or slain in the line of duty. On Thanksgiving, we have handed out turkey dinners and all the fixings to families in the projects. We've even played Santa Claus on Christmas.

The Santa idea started in 1991 when James suggested we go to the post office and grab a stack of letters addressed to the North Pole. We read through them, looked for those gifts we knew a poor mother in the projects couldn't afford, then went shopping. This became a Slick Boys tradition. Every Christmas Eve, we'd load up the squad car and deliver the presents. Because we didn't want anyone to know it was us, we'd leave the gift outside the door, knock, and then hide. I'll never forget the screams of delight from this one little boy in Cabrini after he found the bike he wanted sitting outside his door.

Another time, we had just dropped off a bike to a kid in the Stateway Gardens development when we returned to our car and found it sunk into a pool of water two feet deep. Some gang members standing just inside the building stared at us for a couple minutes, then came over. "Hey, you're the Slick Boys," they said. "You need some help?" The guys lifted the car out of the water. We offered them some money but they shook their heads. "Your money's no good here," they said. So we wished them a Merry Christmas and headed for our next stop.

# 8: Education

# Is Key

*My greatest accomplishment wasn't playing in the NCAA Final Four or even becoming a police officer. My greatest accomplishment was graduating from college.*

—ERIC DAVIS

The three of us agree that education literally saved our lives. Once I left the gang, going to school helped keep me off the streets and got me into college. Having an education lifted James out of the projects and into a productive career. Valuing education enabled Randy to survive the trauma of going to jail and turn it into a meaningful experience.

If having an education could turn us around, it could easily help other kids growing up in the inner city. As soon as we hit the street, we saw that the majority of young men and women we were arresting were high school dropouts. Since then, we have tried to stress the importance of education when we're on the job. Education is the great equalizer, the only true way our poor kids stand a chance of attaining a better life. That's why we came down hard on gang members about making sure that their shorties went to school. After we established a relationship with gang leaders in

ABLA, the first thing we did was work out a deal to make sure the children attended school. If we saw kids on the street during school hours, we threatened to arrest them *and* their leaders. Eventually, kids were proudly showing us their school IDs. "See," they'd say, "I'm in school."

James and I would also spend hours in Cabrini on report card day, handing out dollar bills for every *A* the kids made. And James would make bets with teenage girls about not getting pregnant before they graduated from high school. But these were just gestures. What we really needed to do was to provide kids with the materials and motivation to get an education.

It was the kids themselves who showed us how to do that. In the summer of 1991, we ran into some Cabrini kids headed over to Rush Street to shine shoes. They were trying to make enough money to buy school supplies for that fall. That blew our minds. We decided we had to do something to help these kids and others like them. First, we made a cassette of our Slick Boys rap songs and pedaled them in the projects. When we approached the gangbangers about buying copies, at first they turned us down. We told them, "The money you make should go to these kids, because their mamas gave it to you to buy drugs instead of buying them their school supplies. Now, what are you going to do about this?" Within days, we had sold all 10,000 cassettes. Then, at summer's end, we held a concert behind the police substation and told all the parents to bring their children. There, we handed out nearly 2,000 book bags filled with pencils, notebooks, glue—everything the youngsters needed for school. We still see kids carrying around our book bags, and it always makes us smile like proud parents.

Since then, we've also donated school supplies to the Learning Center in Robert Taylor. This year, we decided that when we travel to schools out of state, instead of collecting our full fee, we will ask the schools to hold a school supply drive. Whatever they collect will go to a school in the inner city. This is also an effective way of bringing people together and making them more aware of each other's differences *and* similarities.

We're also doing that with our Slick Boys program. Our message is simple. We bring a new way of thinking to some old problems.

Using music and humor as well as the kids' own language and style of dress, we try to open up lines of communication between teachers and students, parents and their children, gang members and the police, the inner city and the rest of the nation. We're demonstrating that the best communication is still real, compassionate, human contact.

Here's how a typical Slick Boys program breaks down: We start by sharing our own lives. I tell the story of how I got shot; James talks about growing up in the projects and going to West Point while two of his brothers went to prison; and Randy shares what it was like coming from a large family and losing his parents and several siblings to drugs, cigarettes, and alcohol. With those three stories, we can pretty much cover the experiences of a roomful of kids, no matter what community they come from. The Slick Boys don't talk color, we talk reality.

We also talk to the kids about sex, spirituality, prejudice, and values. James, teaching a lesson about the unimportance of material objects, will bet $100 that the best-dressed kid in the audience is not the smartest. The kids laugh, but James hasn't lost a dollar yet. James says, "We've got to stop thinking that what's important in our community is sex and money. What's important is religion and love. We've got to start working on family, not on popping coochies and making babies. Having kids isn't the same thing as having a family. You've got to be able to *support* those kids."

The issues we discuss and the way we address them often make teachers and parents uncomfortable. It made *me* uncomfortable at first to have to talk about them. But it didn't make me as uncomfortable as going to the funerals of forty-five children under age sixteen in one year, or knowing a thirteen-year-old boy who shot a nine-year-old boy, or visiting a sixteen-year-old kid with AIDS in the hospital. We have to talk about these issues, because if we don't, no one will—not in a way that kids will hear.

We talk the kids' language and so they'll listen to us. It's a simple formula, but it can have a profound impact. Mary Jane Cole is one of the most committed inner-city educators we know. As principal of LaMoyne Grammar School in Chicago, she wiped children's noses when they were sick, sent them to the cafeteria if they didn't have anything to eat before school, and found coats and gloves for them to wear in winter. She knows that it takes a special ability to work effectively with children today.

"All of us educators," Cole says, "with our wonderful plans and concerns, are tuned out a lot of times by our children. We're viewed as authority figures. When a positive message is communicated through something that is popular with kids, it has a much better shot at reaching them. I remember when the Slick Boys performed at my school, Eric asked the kids, 'How many of you have guns in your home?' Hands just shot up. Then from the stage, Eric said to me, 'Mrs. Cole, I think you need to send a note home to your parents.' I did. It was a revelation that so many households had guns and the kids knew where to find them."

Education is the only true key to our childrens' future, especially our poorest children. As a high school sophomore, Florence Canada and her mother knew her education was something she couldn't "afford" to miss. Her mother put her in Catholic school for first and second grades, then she went to public school. In sixth grade, Florence begged her mom to let her go to a private school at the University of Chicago.

"When I saw all the cars everybody's parents were driving, their houses, maids, and jewelry, I was a little envious," Florence says. "It was all I could do to stay in school. I got taken out for a week or two because my mother couldn't pay the tuition bill, and there were school trips and stuff that I couldn't do. After a year, we couldn't afford the school anymore, but I understood. I saw how hard my mother was working to support us and give me the best."

That experience taught Florence what she had to do to get ahead. Back in public school, she was the only seventh-grader in the eighth-grade gifted class. The next year, she was chosen salutatorian and got to speak at graduation. The valedictorian got a ten-speed bike, however, which made Florence mad because she wanted a bike. But she got her revenge: She stayed number one all four years of high school.

We met Florence when we performed as the Slick Boys at her high school in 1994. She approached us afterward, backstage. We were surrounded by students asking for our autographs. Florence was the only one who didn't want us to sign anything. Instead, she wanted us to help her get to a summer program at Stanford University. Once Florence started telling us about herself and her accomplishments, we agreed to sponsor her.

We liked Florence's ambition—after all, that's how the three of us have made it, by taking advantage of any and every chance that came our way. And we liked her toughness about bettering herself—to our minds, the only toughness that counts. Florence simply refused to give in. She never let obstacles like being poor, not having a father, or growing up in a poor neighborhood stand in the way of her education. She encourages others to be just as tough.

"It doesn't really matter what school you go to or where you come from, it's what you get out of that experience," she explains. "There will always be obstacles. Do the best you can in your school but also get yourself out of the neighborhood, find programs, and make friends from other areas."

Today, Florence goes to Washington University in St. Louis. How did she get there? By taking advantage of any program she could find. Every summer she'd do something extra: studying physics, archaeology, and art at a private school; taking writing, math, and TV and radio production courses at Eastern Illinois University; learning about government, speech, and debating at Stanford University as a Junior Statesman of America; and seeing Japan as an exchange student.

By going after her college degree in business and economics, Florence is realizing her dream of one day becoming president of her own corporation, Canada Enterprises. She's got her plan worked out: She'll buy up a number of corporations nationwide, then set her sights worldwide. "I don't want any little mom-and-pop shop," she says. "Those are fine, but that's not what I want. I want corporations." At the rate she's going, we believe she'll get them.

Florence says her mind-set was that because she is black, she couldn't afford *not* to take any opportunity that might help her get where she wanted to go. Working as hard as she does to do her best, Florence shouldn't have to struggle to get money for her education—but she does, and that makes us angry. She has had to piece together a patchwork of partial scholarships. Meanwhile, athletes—both male and female—who put in substantially less time and effort than Florence does, get full scholarship offers from almost every major university in the country. That's sending the message to our kids that academic hard work doesn't really pay off.

Unfortunately, the problem is endemic in our society. In secondary schools as well as colleges, more value is placed on sports than on study. Thousands of our kids pin their hopes on becoming the next Michael Jordan while ignoring their schoolwork. In inner cities, kids get teased or even hurt for being smart. You're at the top of the ladder of respectability in the neighborhood if you're an athlete or a gangster. If you're smart, you're at the bottom. I'm sure there are many talented, really bright kids in our schools who just act middle-of-the-road because they don't want to be stigmatized. I know that's what I did. Fortunately, I was also an athlete and could live in both worlds.

Peer pressure may be the biggest culprit, but parents could neutralize this by stressing to their children the importance of education. That message *has* to come from the top. Only then will it filter down to the children and spread out to the community as a whole. When the Chicago public school system considered cutting the schools' athletic departments during a recent budget crisis, the parents were more up in arms than their children. Frankly, I cheered out loud. Even though athletics played a big role in my life, I now see that I am the person I am today mainly because of my education.

How many of us can name the valedictorian of our high school class? But we all remember the star basketball or football player. As parents, we have to show as much interest in our smart kids as we do in our athletic ones. We have to reward our best and brightest and make education the priority in our schools. We can ultimately raise the level of education in our communities only by stressing the importance of academic achievement in each and every individual home.

A good education starts at home. When a child is born, parents need to begin the educational process as soon as possible. They should stimulate the child intellectually and make him or her hungry for knowledge. Now that his oldest son is about to graduate from high school and go off to college, Randy has been concentrating on his two younger children, Deborah, four, and Marcus, three. "I buy them all the books and preschool materials they need," Randy says. "When they talk, I correct them. I watch *Sesame Street* and *Barney* with them. I encourage them to ask a lot of questions. I want them to grow up always seeking, asking, and striving to know more."

James, who believes that diversity is an important component of education, has his six-year-old son Julian in a multiracial school. It's a year-round school because James wants Julian in a strong and consistent learning environment. "But," James explains, "it's not just the education I send him there for—it's the people value. He's there with Asian kids, Palestinian kids, black kids, white kids, the whole mix."

I truly believe kids would go to school in a refrigerator, if only they were eager enough and prepared to learn. We've been to Cuba and Nigeria. Both are relatively poor countries but they place a high value on education. I think about how my and Randy's parents couldn't go to school because they had to work in the fields and support their brothers and sisters. I think about all the people who fought and died for our right to an equal education. We should be taking advantage of our public school system, if for no other reason than to honor all our people who died wishing they could have gone to school. Instead, we have both high illiteracy and dropout rates. Why?

We could have the best public school system in the world if parents would actively participate in it. Everything that's wrong with the system could be fixed if parents held school officials and public officials more accountable. We are quick to make comments like "Those damn public schools don't teach kids nothing," but have we honestly answered the question "What are *we* doing to teach our kids?"

The problem is that so many parents aren't interested in school themselves, either because they struggled through it or dropped out. As a result, our children are floundering. We've been to primary schools where we've called out a student's name from the tag on his desk and gotten no response. When we asked him his name, he'd say Boo or Stink or some other nickname. The kid didn't know his real name because his parents hadn't bothered to tell him. But if a music video came on TV, that same kid could recite every word. The point is, it's not that these children can't learn; it's that the things they're learning are not conducive to making them productive people. So when a youngster turns fifteen and his parents say they don't know what to do with him, they have only themselves to blame.

When we ask parents how they stress education in their homes, they say, "I tell my kids to get good grades." Fine, we say. But do you give them a safe and clean place to learn? Have you made sure they have all their materials? How often do you stop by their school? Do you sit down with them sometimes and help them with their schoolwork? Do you ask them every night if they have homework, and if they don't, do you give them something to do? The answer we most often get to those questions is no. You'd be surprised at the number of parents we meet who don't even know what grades their children are in or what their teachers' names are.

It doesn't have to be that way. For every dozen parents who don't seem to have a clue, there is at least one like Mark Pratt. Mark is doing an incredible job raising and educating his seven kids in Cabrini-Green. Byrd Elementary is also fortunate to have him as a teacher's assistant, since Mark firmly believes in what he tells all kids: education is the key to getting out of the ghetto.

"My kids all started school at three," Mark says. "They love it because I teach them to love it. My son will tell you that he does more schoolwork at home than he does at school. I'm like, 'You finish your homework? Here.' I give him science, math, reading. I let all my kids flip through my college books. I involved them in the films I made in film school so they could see how films are made. They're working hard to stay on the honor roll so they can get into a gifted program and a good high school.

"Whatever it is they want to do, I'm going to find a way for them to do it. My kids really are my lifeblood. They're what push me on and on. I have to make the dean's list every semester, because I expect them to make the honor roll. They already understand that college is not optional: They're going, even if I have to mortgage my blood. If anything, I'm resourceful. If I don't know something, I'm going to read about it, research it, find out what I need to know. We've just got to be resourceful. We're poor—what more do we have? My babies are going to get everything they need to grow and be successful in life. I've got great plans for them. I see them winning Pulitzers and Nobels."

Parents can make sure that their kids are in instruction programs. But be sure you understand your child's needs. You could send your kid to a basketball camp all summer, but if your kid is a computer whiz, you didn't send him to the right program. Investigate to see if a program is going to meet your child's needs. Know your child. Talk to him. Get involved with some things your child likes.

When parents do take the time to help their kids learn, they often find themselves learning, too. For instance, in my home, my daughter is teaching me a few things. I was basically computer illiterate until Alexandra showed me how to use a PC. Of course, if friends come by, I tell them, "I taught Alexandra everything she knows," but behind closed doors, it's like, "Get that 'Barney' program and let's try it again." I want my daughter to be smarter and go further than I have because I believe each generation should supersede the previous one. My parents dropped out of high school, I graduated from college, and I hope one day Alexandra will go to graduate school.

In the meantime, I'm going to keep learning. I'm learning Spanish now. I also just completed five semesters of education courses, thinking that I might one day teach in school. Like we keep saying, ignorance is a handcuff keeping people locked to poverty and violence. I can't think of anything more satisfying than giving kids the key to unlocking those handcuffs: an education.

# 9: Respect

# One Another

*Helping a community does not just mean painting
apartments, fixing buildings, planting trees, and growing grass. First and foremost, it means raising a person's self-esteem, making him feel better as an
individual. Once what's inside blooms, then the outside
will bloom, too.*

—JAMES MARTIN

When I was in a gang, there were a lot of things I wouldn't do.
It had nothing to do with my fear of the police or the rival gang up
the street; I was afraid of losing the respect of my family. I didn't
want to hurt or dishonor them. So many of the kids we see today
have lost respect for their parents. In turn, they grow up not knowing how to respect other people, even themselves. As a result, we
have a generation of kids growing up with no sense of account-
ability or responsibility to anyone, including themselves. "It's me
against the world," is the prevailing attitude.

A cartoon we have hanging up in our office at Robert Taylor
pretty much sums up how a lot of kids in the projects see their
lives. Two black children are sitting on a stoop, and one says to the

other, "What do you want to be when you grow up?" The other one answers: "Alive."

Death is a daily occurrence in the young lives of the kids we know. As a result, they regularly express sentiments such as, "I live for today; tomorrow's not guaranteed," or "I'm going to die anyway; you can't live forever." We were driving through Cabrini one day after three people had been shot in front of a building known as the Castle. We passed three kids, about fourteen, fifteen, and seventeen, walking past the building. We stopped them. "Where y'all going?" James asked. "Just walking," they replied. When we asked if they were worried about getting shot, they shrugged and said, "If it's your time, it's your time." When the hopes and dreams of our children are killed, it's easy for their bodies to fall.

These young people face a chaotic outside world. Without a strong family background, without one solid parent like Mark Pratt behind them, they are highly vulnerable.

At the heart of improving our families and our communities is respect. It sounds so simple, but it makes so much sense. Just think what would happen if fathers started respecting their children, if children began respecting their parents, if men respected women, if we showed respect to one another, and if each of us respected ourselves. Most negative behaviors that are learned in the home and then acted out in the community would cease if the people heading the house had more self-respect. We're always telling parents that if they mistreat their children, their children will grow up to mistreat someone else or they'll allow someone to mistreat them.

Respect is not a new idea in our communities. But when we think of respect in negative terms like "dissin' " and "disrespect," we misuse and abuse its real meaning. Too many of our young people get killed because somebody "dissed" them or they "disrespected" somebody. A bump, a glare, a word are all it takes for people to start fighting and killing each other. As someone who got shot for precisely this reason, I know that what our black men are dying for has nothing at all to do with respect. The truth is, we would walk away from a confrontation if we had greater respect for ourselves. We would ask ourselves, "Is this worth losing my life over? Isn't my life worth more?" A young man who has respect for himself values his life.

We also have to stop using language that is disrespectful. Violent words often lead to violence. By speaking civilly, we can start to bring civility to our communities. We tell men and women all the time to stop cursing in front of their children. "I have a daughter just like you do," I'll say, "and I'm going to treat her like a lady because I want her to grow up to be a lady." We point out that the words they use among their peers—nigger, bitch, and 'ho—are not words they would want others to say to their kids. Men get upset when the police call them "nigger," yet they've been calling their homeys "nigger" all day. The difference, they say, is that they love their homeys. So we explain, "You might love your parents, too, but do you call them 'nigger'?"

Remember the old adage "Treat people how you want to be treated"? No matter where we go or who we deal with, we treat people with respect. We know that beneath the hard exterior, the battered self-confidence, the "bad" reputation, there is good in a person and the potential to be even better. Everyone wants you to see the good in them. When we look into people's hearts, it's usually the first time anyone has ever really bothered.

Considering how bad it could be, we think a lot of parents in the projects are doing an incredible job of raising their children. A number of mothers and grandmothers are quietly taking care of their families in one of the most challenging—even daunting—environments. We know a single mother in Cabrini who is raising four boys on her own. From their speech and mannerisms alone, you would never guess that they live in a house on a corner nicknamed "Death Row" because of all the people who have died there. They seem more like the kids of a typical two-parent family in the suburbs. Even as young boys, their mother exposed them to the world beyond the projects. Rarely did they play in the neighborhood, and when they did, it was always with each other and usually in their own backyard. Most of the time, they were in church or school or at some cultural event downtown. Now the oldest is in his first year of college, the next attends one of the city's best high schools, and they all have bright futures ahead of them.

There are also fathers who work hard for their kids, men like Mark Pratt, who was one of the first guys in Cabrini to get custody of his kids. A year after he split with the mother of his four oldest children, she unexpectedly left the kids with him one day. At the time, he had neither a decent place nor a decent job, but, Mark says, "It never crossed my mind to give them up."

We moved back into the apartment their mother left. I used to cook our meals on a hot plate, boil water for the kids' baths, and use electric heaters to keep us warm in the winter. I attended PTA meetings at their school and parenting classes at the Women, Infant and Children Clinic, where all the women would turn their heads and ask, "Who is he here with?" I just tried to keep everything as normal as possible.

To me, it's not that hard to raise a family in Cabrini, and it's not that bad a place to grow up. At nineteen, I was in my second year of college but still a part of a gang when my first child came along. Thank God for my son Travonte—he really was the individual who made me as responsible as I am today. I was so determined that I would always be there for him—that I would be everything that my father couldn't be for me—that I left the gang for good. I had planned to take a year off from school to work and get him settled, but, of course, that didn't happen. Now, I'm up to seven kids and a new wife, and I just returned to college last year.

While I feel I've made great strides as a parent, I wasn't quite as prepared as I should have been. Up until 1991, I didn't need welfare because I was getting paid very well when I was working. Since then, most good jobs required a college degree, so I had to fall back on the system. Now I make $14,000 a year as a teacher's assistant and I have medical insurance, but I can't support my family without food stamps. Housing is also a problem. We could have moved from Cabrini, where I pay $125 a month in rent, but I don't want to jump the gun. I don't want to move from apartment to apartment; I really want a home. I'm determined that these kids get a backyard before they're too old.

It's important to mention families like this, because such positive portrayals are usually overlooked whenever there's a discussion about the people who live in public housing. The families that have been torn apart by violence, addiction, and abuse tend to grab all the headlines. They are the ones we, as police officers, come in contact with the most. But the others remind us that flowers can still bloom in the desert.

If we had to identify the root cause of most of the problems confronting the people in the projects, it is the lack of strong family structures and a sense of community. That is what gives rise to gangs, which serve to replace family and community. Drug use, teen pregnancy, and violence itself also thrive in such chaos. As a result, babies like Dantrell are dying. Only after we tackle this problem can we tackle the others.

I remember when parents always watched girls because they didn't want them to get pregnant. Now, I tell parents, "If the worst thing that happens in your family is your daughters get pregnant, at least that's an addition to life." We're seeing so many fourteen- and fifteen-year-old boys killed on the streets of America, it's ridiculous.

Our kids are dying in this country, be it from gang violence, alcoholism, suicide, drug use, or drunk driving. We have a problem with our babies. We all have to face this problem. We need to start reaching out as Americans. Go out into your community, find out where the representatives are, the alderman, the people who are politically connected with your community. Ask about these problems. Get involved in the public school system. Most of the resources are located right around those places. Then, once you find out what the resources are, make a plan. Say, "I'm going to go out and at least take a look."

Maybe come spend the night over here in Cabrini-Green. To learn about housing projects, you can't watch your TV. You have to walk through the halls and smell the urine. You have to go by the playgrounds and see there's nothing for the children to play on. Go by the schools and see there's no knowledge within these schools. Then you can understand the frustrations. Because there is no guarantee that your perfectly raised sons and daughters aren't going to cross paths with those hostile, angry children. They probably will on a daily basis. So, if you're doing fine in your own neighborhood, then go to the next neighborhood where they're not doing so good, and give a helping hand.

According to James, the biggest difference between the projects now and when he was growing up is that there isn't even one strong parental figure in many homes today. Although his mother was a drug addict and his father was never around, James at least had his grandmother to give him the love, guidance, and structure every child needs. He wasn't raising himself. On the other hand, his younger brother Antawaun, who lived with their mother, *did* end up raising himself. He joined a gang and sold drugs. Now he's in prison, like so many other young black men.

Most households we see are like the one Antawaun grew up in. Mama has a drinking problem or she's hooked on drugs or she's barely more than a child herself. Daddy lives with another woman across the way, or he has eleven other children with several different mothers, or he's a winehead. The elders are either no longer in the home or they're scarcely older or wiser than their own children.

That leaves the children to raise not only themselves but often their younger siblings. In a sense, the roles become reversed: The adults act more like children and the children more like adults. The kids are not even allowed the luxury of being children. Instead, they are plunged into adulthood because their parents are too irresponsible to care for them.

One day, on his way home from ABLA, James stopped at a Kentucky Fried Chicken and saw these two little boys standing by the drive-thru.

"Excuse me, sir, do you have some spare change?" one of them asked him.

"Where's your father?" James replied.

"I don't know," he said.

"Where's your mother?"

"I don't know," he answered. "She might be at home."

James asked him, "What does she do?"

He was quiet.

"Does she do that stuff?"

"Yeah," he said.

Then, James asked him what he was planning to do with the money. He said he and his little brother were trying to get something to eat. The boy couldn't have been older than ten, and his brother looked about six. James gave him $20 and said, "Here, don't spend it all at the same time. And don't tell your mother you got it. All she'll do is take it from you." That helped them for today, but what about tomorrow?

Randy says that in Cabrini, the children were truly hungry. Kids would come up to him when he was leaving work after midnight and ask if they could wash his car windows for fifty cents. At all hours of the day, we've seen dozens of children out hustling for money, and not all of them were doing something illegal. We've given countless rides to kids as young as five on their way to the Gold Coast to shine shoes for a buck. They are struggling to get for themselves what their parents should already be providing.

In fact, there are hungry children all over this country. Down in Houston, Texas, Carol and Hurt Porter did something about it. The couple got the idea for Kid-Care, a "meals-on-wheels" program specifically for kids, when they saw children eating out of a Dumpster at a fast-food restaurant. They were so moved they started serving meals they prepared in their own kitchen to homeless families and in housing projects and parks, spending their own paychecks, savings, and even an inheritance on the nonprofit venture. Today, Kid-Care provides about 23,000 meals a month.

Whether it's food, love, or security they're after, children will find some way to get what they need. For too many kids, especially the older ones, that means choosing gangs or drugs. The threat of being locked up no longer deters many of them. Jail has become a respite from their lives back home. At least in jail, they can get three meals a day, a place to sleep, and a social worker to talk to. At home, they can barely get their parents' attention.

Chicago's public housing has to be one of the most difficult places to raise a child. The projects themselves are dirty—the stairwells smell like urine, the elevators are covered with graffiti, the playgrounds are littered with broken glass. The adult residents display an air of futility, of hopelessness, which quickly filters down to the children. In Robert Taylor, where we work now, it's easy to see

143

how this happens. Taylor is in some ways worse than Cabrini, because at least in Cabrini, you can walk a few blocks and end up in downtown Chicago. There's a sense of escape. But in Taylor, which stretches from 40th to 51st Streets on the South Side, you have two miles of nineteen-story buildings with some 12,600 poor people just stacked on top of each other. (And that's not counting all the others who live there but who aren't named on the lease.) At Taylor, there is no escape. All the residents see is drugs, violence, urban decay, and no hope for their future.

Public housing wasn't always in such a mess. When James and I were living in the projects, you could easily get kicked out for violating any one of the many rules—rules the housing authority enforced strictly. CHA even conducted yearly inspections on each apartment. The agency was also more selective about who got apartments back then. You had older people as well as married couples, and a lot of the adults were working. But over the years, as the age and income of the residents have declined, the buildings have steadily deteriorated and crime has grown rampant. In May 1995, the federal government took over running the projects, but by that point, many of the 125,000 residents had already begun to feel as though the city had turned its back on them. The more abandoned they felt, the less they cared about their surroundings and the people in them. And the less concern they showed for their community, the more the city stigmatized and ignored them. It's a vicious cycle that has kept the poorest residents from getting the help they truly need.

Feeling like you'll be trapped forever in the projects is as much psychological as it is real. In Cabrini, children have no idea that they can glimpse the world's fourth-tallest building—the John Hancock Tower—from their homes. In summer, they'll open up the hydrant behind 365 W. Oak and flood the blacktop, but they never walk to Lake Michigan, only a half mile away. In fact, the county jail is the first place outside of the projects that many youngsters growing up in Cabrini will visit. And for those who do venture out, it is a challenge leaving the projects completely behind.

Our biggest concern is the values that have been shaped by the need for survival in the projects, and how these values in turn shape kids growing up there. For a guy, his manhood means every-thing. Obviously, he will get more respect, as a man, for being a big-time gangster than he will for being just another unemployed black man. With so few ways to demonstrate his manhood, one sure way is to make a bunch of babies. Another is to gangbang.

For a lot of young girls, especially those growing up without fa-thers, womanliness is considered their greatest asset. Many of them feel it's all they have to offer. I've had a fifteen-year-old girl come up to me and say, "I really like you. I want to get with you." That's her way of saying I care about you so I want to give you some-thing. I explained to her that, aside from the fact that I am married and have a daughter nearly her age, I am an adult and she is a child.

By the time a girl in the projects is thirteen, she is being pres-sured to have sex, usually by men ten, twenty, even thirty years older. Grown men think nothing of having sex with a young girl, while she will unquestioningly follow the example of her peers and of other women before her. It's all too common that she has her first child by age fourteen or fifteen, drops out of school, becomes an emancipated minor, and gets her own apartment. So the cycle continues.

We believe that the key to rebuilding our families is teaching parents to *be* parents. If we can rebuild our families by educating the parents, that would go a long way toward breaking that cycle and solving most of the problems in public housing. Most parents, deep down, really do love their children and want the best for them, though they may not know how to show it. As fathers our-selves, we can sympathize with what parents go through. We may not know any more than any other parent, but if we have some in-formation that might be helpful, we're going to share it.

The first step in helping families function as true families is get-ting fathers back in the home. In Cabrini, because their kids lived in another building in hostile territory, many young fathers had just about given up on seeing their children. We had to set up the gang peace treaty so the young men would stop fighting. This allowed many fathers to be reunited with their children for the first time in years.

145

The one thing these guys had a lot of was time. In general, society measures fathers by what they can provide financially for their families. So many men in our communities aren't working, we no longer considered that as a criterion for manhood. But what they did have to give their kids was time—more than twice the time other fathers had to give. We told them that in the long run, time would be worth more to their children than money. We suggested they watch their children while the mothers went to work. When they grumbled about being baby-sitters, we reminded them that they were fulfilling their responsibility as fathers.

Of course, that's not to say we don't want fathers working. We've helped anywhere from fifty to a hundred men and women in the projects get jobs, while sending another two hundred back to school for their high school equivalency diploma. When men and women are educated, they're more comfortable spending time at home. They aren't embarrassed when their children ask them to help with their homework. And they can get a job and start providing for their families.

Having a job gives not only the father but the entire family a sense of worth and pride. Even if the job is menial, the children can appreciate that their father works hard for them. In turn, the father can expect his children to work hard, too, and also bring pride to the family. With high expectations at home, a son is less likely to join a gang and a young daughter will avoid getting pregnant.

One of the most important things parents can do for their children is to be good role models. A role model does not have to be a basketball player or a movie star, just ordinary Joes like us. Each one of us has a gift we can share with our children. I inherited my compassion from my father and I hope to pass it on to my daughter. James got his strong desire to give back from his grandmother and plans to instill the same value in his son. And Randy picked up his father's work ethic, which he passed on to Randy Jr., who works, goes to school, and plays basketball. Moms and dads who get up at six every morning to go to a job are showing their children the importance of hard work. If they hang out in the building lobby late at night, their children will pick up on that, too. Whatever we do becomes a powerful example to our children.

Like a lot of kids in the projects, Vino Simmons didn't get much guidance growing up. His mom was never home and he only saw his father a few times a year. At fourteen, he had his first child by a woman who was twenty. Now, he's thirty-three and has sixteen children, and thirteen of them have different mothers. "I have big regrets for how all of them were raised," Vino says. "It wasn't like I abandoned them, but the things I was doing, I didn't want my family to be around."

Vino had no idea of how to set an example for his own kids. Sadly, his oldest son is continuing the cycle as a gangbanger. Recently, some guys broke his jaw. Vino says, "I try to talk to him, but he looks at me like I'm a chump. He's still stuck on who I used to be. When he was growing up, he could call his daddy and have ten guys come to school and pick him up in a Cadillac. Or he could call his daddy and have a guy jacked up. Now, he wants to be the baddest thing. I hate to think about the way he's going. I let him get too far away from me."

Vino now realizes that being a father means more than just making a baby and providing for him or her financially. Having a strong sense of responsibility really is the best contraceptive. Once a man is fully responsible for his child and realizes the amount of time and effort it takes to care for him or her, he will think before having another. Vino has moved in with the mother of his three youngest children and is taking an active role in their lives. Parents have to make the same vow to our children that we make to our spouses: I will take care of you for better or for worse. We must stand by our children.

We tell young mothers and fathers that being poor doesn't mean you can't be a good parent. Being poor doesn't give you permission to become a dope fiend or an alcoholic. It doesn't excuse you from reading a book to your children or sitting down at the table to have dinner with them. Children's most basic needs—love and caring communication—don't cost anything.

But showing emotion can be very difficult, especially for people in poor communities, where having feelings is seen as a sign of vulnerability or weakness. Everyone is trying to show how hard and tough they are. I can be sitting with a group of gang members and say, "Man, I'm tired of all this killing." The only responses I'll hear are, "A man's got to do what a man's got to do," or "You goin' die, you goin' die." So I'll go up to big, strong gangbangers, and give them hugs and kisses and tell them I love them, because I know they need that. A lot of them can't even remember the last time their mothers kissed them. I think of one gang member, Rodnell Dennis, who, at age twelve, was sentenced to thirty-nine years in prison for shooting a nine-year-old. Rodnell's mother wore herself out whipping him. What difference would it have made in his life if she had told him she loved him *before* he went to prison?

"Some people in Cabrini don't even know what love is," Rod says. "The way you show love is by telling your child 'I love you.' My mom never told me she loved me till I got in jail. I was talking to her on the phone, and when I got ready to hang up, I was like, 'Ma.' She was like, 'What?' 'I love you,' I said. And she told me, 'I love you, too.' That's how it started. The first time she told me, it felt so good I thought about it all night. *All night.*"

Once we help people to rebuild their families, then we can take the next step: getting them off public assistance. When word came down about welfare reform, residents told us, "Crime is going to go up; homelessness is going to get worse." "Do you hear your slave mentality?" I shot back. When slavery ended, many slaves never left the plantation, because that was all they knew. Having a roof over their head and enough food to eat meant more to them than having their freedom. The same thing is happening now. President Clinton and the Congress are removing the shackles of public aid from the poor. But instead of looking at this as an opportunity to grow, many African Americans see it as a setback.

We don't. We welcome the changes in public housing and welfare. One of the most pernicious dependencies we as black people have is the dependency on public aid. This is not a problem exclusive to blacks—there are actually more white people on the welfare rolls—but the problem for blacks is made worse because of racism. Our opportunities are already limited because of our skin color; when we add poverty to the mix, it's easy to give up and think that we are worthless, that we can't do more than collect a welfare check. And when we adopt that mind-set, it's easy to pick up the bottle or turn to drugs and let go of hope.

For years, we've been trying to wake our people up to the reality of where the country is headed. Before the truce in Cabrini, we pointed out to the gang members that the buildings they were fighting over didn't belong to them and that one day they might have to leave. "Oh, no," came the response, "they're not going to do that to us." Since then, six buildings have been torn down—with more sure to follow—in order to make way for a private development of mixed-income townhouses. Thousands of residents have already been turned out of their apartments. Similar changes are happening in several other project developments in the city, generally in places where the buildings occupy valuable real estate. And while residents are screaming and pointing fingers at the politicians and the real-estate developers, the blame for their predicament rests squarely on their own shoulders. These buildings weren't taken from them—they gave them away.

Had the residents been able to put aside their petty differences and come together to form a single, powerful voice, they might have had more say in how their development was run. They might have had the opportunity to purchase their buildings, bring in businesses, and create a true community. It would have been difficult for the city to bulldoze a community that was united and committed to growth. But sometimes it takes a real kick in the butt for people to wake up.

We want to start a new attitude in our poor black communities, one that values hard work. Right now, in Robert Taylor, we're preparing adults to go out and get jobs. Working with our commander, we have turned the old battered women's shelter above the police station into a learning center, complete with computers, GED classes, a nursery, and a fitness center. We're giving young men and women the skills they need to construct a better life for themselves. It's no quick fix, but, like my mom always said, "You can feed a man a fish and he'll eat for a day or you can teach him how to fish and he'll eat for a lifetime." We're "raising" adults to be independent so that they can do the same for their kids and finally break the welfare cycle.

Our center is conveniently located, so residents can walk to it; it's multipurpose, so that we can address all the needs of a person; and it's free. So far, about 125 people use the center each day, and we're rounding up more people every time we walk through the development. We're doing what a real brother—and a real father—does: forcing people to get on their feet and accept responsibility for their own lives. We already believe in them; now we just have to get them to believe in themselves. People don't want handouts—they want an opportunity to help themselves make better lives.

# 10: Help People

# One by One,

# One to One

*Each of us came on the job thinking, "Man, I'm going to go out there and save the world." We figured out pretty quickly that we alone couldn't save the whole world— but we could try to save pieces of it.*

Each one of us was helped in some way by someone else. It's what kept us from going the route of the people we arrest. We know deep in our hearts that reaching out to help someone, especially a child, is the greatest gift we as individuals can give to one another.

Taking care of our children is the most important thing we can do. I'm not talking about me alone taking care of my daughter or you alone taking care of your children. I'm talking about *us,* as a nation, coming together to make a concerted effort right now to take care of all our children—black, white, Latino, Asian, poor, rich, every last one of them. We have adopted this principle so that wherever we go, we try to take every child as our own. Every child we come in contact with, we give at least a minute of our time. We learn that child's name, ask him if he did his homework today, or ask her how her mama's doing. When we visit a school, we sign every autograph, answer every question, listen to every problem. We stay for as long as the kids need us.

Not too long ago, after a show at a high school, a girl came up to Randy and said she wanted to talk to someone. "I didn't want to say this in front of the whole class," she said. "I've been getting a lot of flack about this. I was raped by five boys who are here today. What should I do?"

Randy says, "There was no way I could say, 'I understand how you feel.' No way. So I called over one of our dancers, Elaine, who had told me that she had been raped as a young girl. I let them talk. Now all three of us were standing there crying. I could relate to the hurt and the pain that she was going through, even though I wasn't the one she needed to talk to. Elaine and the girl talked to an assistant principal, who ended up getting the police involved. They brought all five boys in and the case is in the court system. Elaine still corresponds with the girl regularly."

When I was growing up, there was always one woman in the neighborhood we called Nosey Miss So and So. If a bunch of us were standing on the corner, she would ask us what we were doing. If she didn't recognize someone, she would ask him why he was in her neighborhood. Now we live in a time when neighbors don't know one another, when adults are afraid to talk to children, and children run the neighborhood. In places like those, whether it's a poor or an upscale neighborhood, gangs and crime will flourish. But if communities came together, we wouldn't have such problems. It seems ironic to me that today we have all these modes for communication—the television, the newspaper, the computer—yet we're forgetting the most important way to communicate, and that is face-to-face. We have to get out of our homes more and leave our jobs earlier so that we can start talking to our neighbors again.

We don't need more government intervention to solve our children's problems; we need *community* intervention. Of course, the federal government must do its part, but we think more private citizens, like Trudy Able Peterson Hofler, need to step up, too. In 1984, she started a pilot program in New York City to help determine exactly how many "throw away" kids were on the street. In the process of counting, she began to know the kids as individuals and sought funding, which quickly reached $1 million, to actually help them. Because she recognized that most of the kids had lost trust in the social services system, she took to mentoring and counseling them in their own environment—on the street, around the clock. In addition to her StreetOutreach program, she and her staff organized a drop-in center where the kids can take a shower, get some privacy, eat, or meet with a counselor as they cross the bridge back to traditional lives. The StreetOutreach program develops careful, slow relationships that help kids prepare to make healthier choices.

In Kansas City, Missouri, the Safe Place program is hosted by a convenience-store chain whose directors recognized that kids flocked to the city's quick-marts for candy and soda pop. Employees in each store hand out business cards that advertise the Safe Place program, and offer kids a 29-cent refill on drinks (so the cards will stay in their pockets). If a child is in trouble at home, wants to avoid riding with drinkers, or is being harassed or followed on the streets, he knows that he can wait at the store until a trained shelter volunteer or parent comes to pick him up. While the safety benefits of the program are obvious, the organizers say the kids also learn that they have sensible choices and alternatives, and that it gives youth who are only beginning to have problems a chance to get help early.

We think everyone should put in their time to save a piece of the world. If you can't give your time, the least you can do is financially support a person or program. Check the list of organizations on page 163 to get started right now.

It really comes back to thinking about people as individuals rather than lumping them together in categories such as "losers" or "welfare mothers." Sometimes all a person needs is an extra push. Marva Roland, for instance, was living in Cabrini and headed in the wrong direction when we first met her. She was nineteen, pregnant with her first child, and going with a guy who sold drugs. We raided her boyfriend's place, knocked the door down, put everybody in handcuffs, and walked them all across a field. Because it was her first offense, Marva got eighteen months probation. "Still,"

Marva recalls, "I kept on hanging around that wild crowd, got pregnant with my second child, and caught a gun case. The judge threw the case out and told me I better not appear before him again."

"You're too smart for this, Marva," Eric would say to me. One day, he told me he had found an apartment for me. A lot of people are scared of the challenge of living outside the projects, but I knew this was not the life for me and my two little boys. I moved out, even though my rent was $360 and my aid check was $371. I struggled for about a year until Eric also found me a job at his mother's bar and restaurant.

Now I live in an apartment on the South Side. I fully support my boys by working as a hostess at a jazz club. Eric is the only positive male role model my kids have. Every week he comes to visit them. He takes them to get their hair cut and he tells them right from wrong. When Tyrese stole some sparklers from Woolworth's on July 3, Eric came and tore his butt up. When the school tells me Tyrese is running up and down the bus or something, I just call Eric. I dropped out of school in the eleventh grade, but I've promised Eric I'm going to go back.

If Eric and the Slick Boys hadn't given me a hand, I would still be in Cabrini. They were really taking a chance. Now, I just forget that they are the police. I trust them like they are friends.

That's what we mean by working one-to-one. Each one who is helped in turn helps another. As Mark Pratt says, "Everyone here has to make the decision to reach somebody else."

Mark practices what he preaches. He has tutored thirty-five girls at the youth center in Cabrini and started a dance troupe that traveled all over the city, winning awards. Close to half of those young women went to college and have graduated and/or are working. Only three got pregnant at an early age, and of those, two got married and all three finished high school. As editor of a newspaper he helped start in Cabrini and as lead plaintiff in the lawsuit against the city to stop the police sweeps in the projects, Mark became known as the Mayor of Cabrini. Four or five guys call him regularly from the penitentiary, and they talk about everything, including the decisions that led them to the gangs and prison. He's also helping younger boys still in the community find the confidence to leave the gangs.

Another individual we admire is Al Carter. He has run a youth foundation in Cabrini for twenty years, starting out in 1117 Cleveland, the building known as the Castle. He helped raise a generation of children through his basketball and baseball programs, and now he's doing the same for *their* children. Al teaches more than just good sportsmanship; he instructs the kids on how to carry themselves, stresses education, and provides constant discipline and support.

Marian Nzinga Stamps remains one of the most special people we've ever met. A former Black Panther, Marian earned the title Mama of Cabrini by pushing tenants' rights and community control of education within the projects. She helped get Sojourner Truth and Schiller schools built in Cabrini-Green, and, along with other Chicago Panthers, started her own collective and school within the development. She moved out of the projects in 1977, but she didn't forget Cabrini. Besides resolving disputes among residents, including bringing together the different gangs to form a truce, she went head-to-head with city officials every time they threatened the well-being of people in Cabrini. She even stopped the city from tearing down the building where she used to live by standing in front of a bulldozer. She worked nearby at the Winfield Moody Health Clinic, where she spearheaded an outreach program to cut down on the number of black infant deaths.

A few years ago, Marian decided she was tired and was going to move back to her hometown in Mississippi. She never made it. At age fifty-two, she had a heart attack and died. Marian had her enemies, including the police who called her "Mama Stone" and "Queen of the Cobras," because they thought she was a gang leader. But, judging from the politicians, activists, gang members, and public housing residents who attended her funeral, Marian had a lot of supporters as well. We hope to carry on her work by giving whatever assistance we can to the five daughters she left behind.

What all of these people have in common is their desire to do something about making their piece of the world a better place.

There are many, many other people and programs we think do good work. Twenty-first Century Vote is a political organization started by the Black Gangster Disciples in Chicago. Although it's controversial, we think the leaders are doing a great job working with the gangs and getting beefs solved peaceably.

Film star Sharon Stone has a program in Los Angeles called Planet Hope, which provides shelter and support for homeless girls who have children. She has involved her whole family in making the program work, and, from what we've seen, it does.

In Yonkers, New York, the directors of Big Brothers–Big Sisters run a six-week summer program to give girls a safe, constructive place while they are out of school. As part of the program, the eighth-grade girls draw imaginary jobs out of a hat, and then learn how to manage the salary and a checkbook. Each girl is given a mailbox, and every few days she receives utility bills and random expenses like an emergency car repair or doctor bill. Occasionally, she even receives windfalls or bonuses. At the end of each week, every girl "spends" her savings—if there are any—on items from a mail-order catalog. In addition to teaching the girls practical skills, it also helps them learn the value of jobs with higher salaries.

Another organization we like is Facing History and Ourselves. Started by a former educator in Boston, it goes right to the core of people's prejudice by bringing people from different ethnic groups into contact with one another to talk about their experiences. Jewish people talk about the Holocaust. Black people who grew up in the inner city talk about the Civil Rights movement. Hispanic people who are just coming to this country talk about how they're treated. Others discuss being white and poor in America. When you don't interact with people from different backgrounds or religions, you tend to start coming up with your own opinions or adopting the opinions of the community that you live in—which are usually wrong. When representatives of these groups actually come speak to you in person, they become human beings.

I went to West Roxbury, Massachusetts, a predominantly Irish and Italian community, as part of Facing History and Ourselves. I initially thought, *What do I have to talk to these people about?* But I talked about the American dream. We all have problems. In an affluent home, it could be abandonment and alcoholism and drug abuse. Those problems are as large to them as my gang problems were to me.

I spoke with probably 2,000 kids that day. They weren't thinking, *Well, I'm not in a gang. That doesn't have anything to do with me;* they were saying, "He dealt with his problems and I can deal with my problems the same way." The kids all went home at lunch and their parents had never seen their kids this excited. They wanted me to go back that night so they could hear exactly what this guy talked to their kids about.

If I'd had in my own mind the picture of what racism looks like, it was that auditorium filled with parents that night. I said, "You know, it's easy to see that many of you are Italian and Irish and I'm black. Those are the easy things that we can see. But you know what? I hope my kid grows up and goes to Harvard and becomes a lawyer or a doctor and helps out this society."

No one in that audience could say they wanted anything different for their kids. They realized, "We're parents in this audience. And he is a parent, too." If they saw my black kid playing football in the street in West Roxbury, I want them to tell him to stop because it's dangerous. Otherwise, they're not responsible parents. We have to take care of *all* our children.

We are just three regular guys who said we wanted to make a difference. We didn't know how, but we figured it out as we went along. By helping a few young men, we actually reach other men, women, and children. Using our lives as example, we are able to give young people hope and guidance. I realize how lucky the three of us have been. As many violent situations, shoot-outs, and drug busts as we've been in, it's a wonder none of us has ever taken a bullet. God has obviously put a hand around us so that we can fulfill our mission in life.

The principles we have talked about in this book—hope, understanding, and respect—guide us through our work in the projects, but their value goes beyond life in the inner city. As a nation, we have to stop saying, "I took care of mine, now you take care of yours," because that will simply get us nowhere. The problems of our children are not only the responsibility of blacks or Latinos or poor people to fix. Drugs and violence are not unique to the projects and the inner city. Gang activity is rising in rural and suburban areas for some of the same reasons you see it in the inner city: the breakdown of the family and community, the glamorization of gangsterism, and the money that crime—specifically drugs—generates. These are American problems that must be solved by all Americans. If we don't deal with the problems of our poorest people, we will pay the price as a nation. Not only will crime and poverty increase, but we will lose this country's greatest asset—the potential of its citizens.

If reading our book leaves you with a better awareness of your role in your community and your country, if you are inspired to help yourself or empowered to help others, we've done what we set out to do.

# Epilogue

Today, we work throughout Chicago in all of its housing projects. Our job is to drive around, talk to people, and keep the peace. We work out little squabbles before they turn into bigger fights. We're like police diplomats. Recently, the peace treaty we had helped set up at Cabrini started to break down. One gang, the Mickey Cobras, all lived in a building that was slated for demolition. They had to relocate to buildings where their arch enemies, the Black Gangster Disciples, hung out. There was tension and it was about to erupt. Well, we couldn't let something as crazy as redevelopment destroy all the hard work we had done to make sure that people could go to school, get jobs, and have a peaceful community. And when I say "we," I'm not just talking about only our efforts as Slick Boys—I'm talking about everybody who had helped: the gangs themselves, the elders, the churches, the police department.

So we went down and talked to the bosses. Once again, there is peace in Cabrini. For how long? We don't know. When someone asks us if we get discouraged, we say, "Look, the gang fights lasted ten years. We've been Slick Boys for five years. In another five years, we hope there won't be a need for the Slick Boys anymore."

The cycle will be broken by a generation of people who will say, "I'm going to abide by this new way of thinking. I'm going to get up. I'm going to go to work." A generation of kids who will have grown up learning and living to serve and protect. To speak the language. To have big expectations. To give something back. To be a ray of hope. To lead by example. To not play to the stereotypes. To get an education. To respect one another.

To help each other one by one, one to one.

# Four:

# Making a Difference

# Helpful

# Organizations

Once you decide you would like to do something concrete in your piece of the world—or support a program that does—there are hundreds of places you can contact. To help you find out more, we offer the following list of community organizations, large and small, local and national. They represent a variety of political and religious orientations, but they all are dedicated to helping people, especially youth. They are committed to turning formerly hopeless lives into lives of health, wholeness, and achievement.

You can too.

## ADVOCATES FOR YOUTH

1025 Vermont Avenue NW, Suite 200
Washington, DC 20005
(202) 347-5700
Kate Fothergill

Dedicated to increasing the opportunities for and abilities of youth to make healthy decisions about sexuality. The organization provides information and education to professionals, policy makers, the media, and youth advocacy agencies.

ALATEEN

Al-Anon Family Group Headquarters
1600 Corporate Landing Parkway
Virginia Beach, VA 23454
(800) 356-9996; (804) 563-1600
World Directory Meeting Line: (800) 344-2666
Web site: www.alateen.org

For young people whose lives have been affected by someone else's alcohol problems. Members are taught that they are not the cause of anyone else's drinking, that they cannot change or control the behavior of someone else. Alateen works to give these young people the intellectual and spiritual resources to cope, develop their own potential, and build satisfying and rewarding lives. The meetings are conducted by the young people themselves, guided by an adult Al-Anon member, and are designed to allow members to share experiences, hope, and strength.

ALLIANCE FOR PARENTAL INVOLVEMENT IN
    EDUCATION

P.O. Box 59
East Chatham, NY 12060
(518) 392-6900
Seth Rockmuller

Parent network helping parents explore educational options, including public, private, and home schooling. In addition to a newsletter, ALLPIE publishes pamphlets on educational options and parents' rights. The organization sponsors workshops, retreats, and an annual family conference. Educational books and additional materials are available through ALLPIE's mail order lending library and through its Book and Resources Catalog.

Helpful Organizations

## ALTERNATIVES FOR VIOLENCE

P.O. Box 300431
Houston, TX 77230
(713) 747-9999
Marjorie Kerr, Executive Director

A volunteer organization that operates 1,000 workshops annually in forty states for community and youth groups and prison inmates. The focus is on strengthening conflict-resolution skills by identifying the causes of violence (anger, fear, feelings of powerlessness) and offering alternatives such as affirmation, compromise, and cooperation.

## AMERICAN FRIENDS SERVICE COMMITTEE YOUTH PROGRAMS

1501 Cherry Street
Philadelphia, PA 19102
(215) 241-7295
Helene Pollock, Recruitment Coordinator

Summer program for volunteers eighteen to twenty-six years old who work with villagers and community leaders in Mexico under the direction of a local Mexican organization, building schools and assisting with agricultural projects. Those who participate must speak Spanish and pay for the cost of travel, training, insurance, food, and accommodations. Scholarships are available. (Application deadline: April 1.)

## AMERICAN HUMANICS

4601 Madison Avenue
Kansas City, MO 64112
(816) 561-6415
Dr. Kirk G. Alliman, President

Offers leadership training for professional employment in youth agencies. The curriculum is used in seventeen American colleges and universities. Publishes *Humanics: The Journal of Leadership for Youth and Human Services.*

## AMERICAN RED CROSS

Division of Youth Involvement
8111 Gatehouse Road
Falls Church, VA 22042
(703) 206-6000
E-mail: Speaks R@usa.red-cross.org
Web site: www.redcross.org
Ron Speaks, Director, Youth Involvement

Sponsors a variety of volunteer and community-service programs through 1,400 local chapters nationwide to encourage youth development. For more information, contact a local chapter listed in the phone book, or use the locator found on the Web site.

## AMERICA'S PRIDE PROGRAM

National Parents' Resource Institute for Drug Education
3610 Dekalb Technology Parkway, Suite 105
Atlanta, GA 30340
(770) 458-9900
Web site: www.prideusa.org
Michelle Basket, National Youth Director

Provides a wide variety of drug-prevention programs and services to parents, youth, community organizations, and educators in the United States and in twenty-nine other countries. Sponsors weekend retreats designed to instill the value of education, communication, and leadership.

Helpful Organizations

AMERICAN YOUTH FOUNDATION

1315 Ann Avenue
St. Louis, MO 63104
(314) 772-8626
Pat Jones, Vice President of Conferences
Mark Pawlowski, Vice President, Camping Programs

Offers school- and community-based leadership training to young people in preparation for careers in youth organizations. Sponsors year-round programs in several U.S. cities and summer camp programs in Michigan, New Hampshire, and California.

AMERICAN YOUTH WORK CENTER

1200 17th Street NW, 4th floor
Washington, DC 20036
(202) 785-0764
Terry Kush, Administrative Office

Provides information, training, publications, advocacy, and international exchange opportunities for youth workers. Publishes *Youth Today—The Newspaper on Youth Work,* a bimonthly publication, and a variety of brochures.

ASPIRA ASSOCIATION

1444 I Street NW, 8th floor
Washington, DC 20005
(202) 835-3600
E-mail: aspira@aol.com
Ronald Blackbern-Moreno, President

National nonprofit organization serving Puerto Rican and other Latino youth and their families through leadership, education, and advocacy. Community-service programs include mentoring and after-school activities. Publications available include training manu-

167

als; fact sheets on Hispanic health, education, and violence; and a quarterly newsletter.

## BARRIOS UNIDOS / CALIFORNIA COALITION TO END BARRIO WARFARE

313 Front Street
Santa Cruz, CA 95060
(408) 457-8208
Daniel Alejandrez, Director

A statewide organization with local chapters committed to helping young people make healthy decisions regarding their lives and their community.

## BERNAL HEIGHTS NEIGHBORHOOD CENTER

515 Cortland Street
San Francisco, CA 94110
(415) 206-2154

Provides youth employment and training; a gang-prevention program; senior services; a number of cultural activites and events, including the annual Fiesta on the Hill; and ongoing community organizing within the Bernal community.

## BIG BROTHER ASSOCIATION OF GREATER BOSTON

286 Congress Street
Boston, MA 02210
(617) 542-9090

Provides mentors to boys seven to thirteen years old who have no fathers at home.

BIG BROTHERS / BIG SISTERS OF AMERICA

230 N. 13th Street
Philadelphia, PA 19107
(215) 567-7000
E-mail: BBBSA@aol.com

Matches children, mostly from single-parent homes, with caring adult mentors and role models. The one-on-one relationships are supervised by professional caseworkers. Also available are counseling, referral, and family-support services and drug abuse, adolescent pregnancy, and juvenile delinquency prevention programs.

BIG SISTER ASSOCIATION OF GREATER BOSTON

161 Massachusetts Avenue
Boston, MA 02115
(617) 236-8060

Provides mentors and role models for girls seven to fifteen years old and for girls up to age twenty who are pregnant or parenting.

B'NAI B'RITH YOUTH ORGANIZATION

1640 Rhode Island Avenue NW
Washington, DC 20036
(202) 857-6639
Melanie Weiner

An international organization for Jewish adolescents that strives to develop leadership and personal growth through programs such as Project E.A.R.T.H. (Everyone Has A Responsibility To Our Home) and Project R.E.A.C.H. (Responsibility Everywhere to Aid and Care for the Homeless).

MAKING A DIFFERENCE

BOSTON PARTNERS IN EDUCATION

145 South Street
Boston, MA 02111
(617) 451-6145
Joyna Bozzotto

Volunteers act as mentors, tutor, and read aloud to Boston public school students.


BOYS & GIRLS CLUBS OF AMERICA

1230 W. Peachtree Street NW
Atlanta, GA 30309
(404) 815-5758
Judith J. Carter, Senior Vice President, Program Services

The nation's largest youth service organization. Programs in 1,900 clubs in the United States, Puerto Rico, and the Virgin Islands include social recreation, citizenship and leadership development, cultural enrichment, health and physical education, personal and educational development, and outdoor and environmental education. The focus is directed to young people from disadvantaged backgrounds.


BOYS TOWN NATIONAL HOTLINE

(800) 448-3000

A 24-hour hotline for boys, girls, and their parents in crisis.


BOYS TOWN NATIONAL RESOURCE AND TRAINING CENTER

14100 Crawford
Boys Town, NE 68010
(800) 545-5771, ext. 100

Offers affordable workshops and training for youth-care workers and educators and provides on-site training, consultation, and evaluation services. Workshops have included Working with Aggressive Youth, Teaching Social Skills to Youth, and Administrative Intervention.

THE BRIDGE FOR KIDS

1387 Oak Street
San Francisco, CA 94117
(415) 522-0100
Randy Newcomb

Provides in-home respite child care and help for families with members who are affected or infected with AIDS.

BUILDERS CLUB

Kiwanis International
3636 Woodview Trace
Indianapolis, IN 46268
(800) 549-2647; (317) 875-8755
Dave Wohler, Manager

Leadership development and community-service program that operates through middle schools.

BUSINESS PROFESSIONALS OF AMERICA

5454 Cleveland Avenue
Columbus, OH 43231
(614) 895-7277
Gary L. Hannah, President and CEO

Promotes leadership, citizenship, and academic and technical skills among middle and secondary school students, and provides networking opportunities for students and businesspeople.

MAKING A DIFFERENCE

CAMBRIDGE COMMUNITY SERVICES
99 Bishop Allen Drive
Cambridge, MA 02139
(617) 876-5214
Susan Goldman

Provides mentoring to teenage parents in making decisions about education, career choices, and goals.

CAMPUS OUTREACH OPPORTUNITY LEAGUE
1511 K Street NW, Suite 307
Washington, DC 20005
(202) 637-7004
E-mail: homeoffice@cool2serve.org
Web site: www.cool2serve.org
Melissa Kendrick, Executive Director

Recent college graduates and students operate this national non-profit organization, which works to improve student involvement in community service through training and education.

CATHOLIC BIG BROTHERS OF NEW YORK
45 E. 20th Street
New York, NY 10003
(212) 477-2250
Sandy Maskell, Program Director

Adult mentors serve as friends and role models to inner-city youth ages nine to seventeen, mostly from single-parent families. Catholic Big Brother / Big Sister programs operate in other U.S. cities as well. For further information, contact the Catholic archdiocese office in your area.

172

Helpful Organizations

CENTER FOR ADOLESCENT STUDIES

School of Education
Indiana University
201 North Rose
Bloomington, IN 47405
(812) 856-8321
E-mail: Ingersol@indiana.edu
Gary Ingersoll

Works to meet the social and emotional growth and development needs of adolescents by providing support to adults working with youth, investigating current social issues, and providing tools for teens to learn and practice new, healthy behaviors. Services include Drug Information Assessment and Decision Support, a computer-based decision aide to help schools select the drug-prevention program most likely to meet their needs; Institute on Adolescents at Risk, a workshop that teaches skills to deal with teen risk-taking and crisis intervention; and advice, strategies, and lesson plans for secondary-school teachers who want to enhance the social and emotional growth of their students.

CENTER FOR CHILD WELFARE

George Mason University
4400 University Drive MS 2E8
Fairfax, VA 22030
(703) 993-1951
Ruth E. Zambrana

Dedicated to promoting and advancing interdisciplinary knowledge and policy in child, youth, and family welfare, with a focus on Hispanic/Latino children, youth, and families at risk in Latin America and the United States. The Center conducts research, disseminates information and materials, and provides training.

## THE CENTER FOR DEMOCRACY AND CITIZENSHIP

Humphrey Institute
301 19th Avenue S
Minneapolis, MN 55455
(612) 625-0142
Harry C. Boyte, Director

Works to promote democracy, strengthen citizenship and civic education, and get young people involved in government and public work through outreach, community interaction, and research projects.

## CENTER FOR HUMAN RESOURCES

Heller Graduate School
Brandeis University
60 Turner Street
Waltham, MA 02154
(617) 736-3770
E-mail: HN3676@Handsnet.org
Susan Curnan, Director

Nationally recognized research, professional development, policy, and program-development center working in the fields of youth development, education, employment, and community development. Provides training and technical assistance to policy makers, program managers, and line staff on youth and community issues, including school-to-work system development, work-based learning, employability assessment and case management, and development of comprehensive, communitywide partnerships. The Center also conducts program evaluations and operates the Youth Development Forum, an online clearinghouse at www.handsnet.org.

CENTER FOR INTERGENERATIONAL LEARNING

Temple University
1601 N. Broad Street, Room 206
Philadelphia, PA 19122
(215) 204-6970
Nancy Z. Henkin, Ph.D., Executive Director

Serves as a national resource for intergenerational programming by developing cross-age programs, providing training and
technical assistance, and disseminating intergenerational educational materials. Programs include drug prevention; child development training for adults fifty-five years and older; a volunteer
program for older adults to work in elementary schools; a program in which older adults provide in-home support to families
of children with disabilities and chronic illnesses; intergenerational theater program support services for children being raised
by grandparents; Homefriends, a child neglect prevention program, through which families of children with special needs receive in-home support from older volunteers; intergenerational
retreats; and a program in which college students teach English to
elderly refugees and immigrants.

CENTRAL UNION MISSION / CAMP BENNETT

20501 Georgia Avenue
Brookeville, MD 20833
(301) 774-4420
Steve Hoey

Offers a camping program for inner-city children.

THE CHAPIN HALL CENTER FOR CHILDREN AT THE
UNIVERSITY OF CHICAGO

1313 E. 60th Street
Chicago, IL 60637

(312) 753-5900
Renae Ogletree, Senior Research Associate

A $30 million initiative in eight Chicago communities is testing the center's theory that services should develop children's potential instead of preventing or solving problems. Child welfare agencies and the juvenile justice system are using services like organized sports, religious youth groups, parks, libraries, and community centers to improve the quality of life for children and youth.


CHEROKEE NATION

Education and Human Services Division
P.O. Box 948
Tahlequah, OK 74465
(918) 456-0671
Londa Cox, Department Manager, Tribal Services Department
    Youth Programs
Larry Ketcher, Department Director, Cherokee Nation Youth Fair
    Chance

Offers a variety of services for Cherokee young people: a program for Cherokee youth sixteen to twenty-one years old eases transition to the workforce; the Summer Youth Employment Program; an annual Indian Youth Vocational Conference, which introduces participants to different careers and vocations; a Summer Youth Tribal Internship program, which offers opportunities to work in a professional setting; Cherokee Nation Youth Fair Chance, a program in Oklahoma that promotes education and seeks to reduce dropout rates and increase enrollment on the college level by offering employment training and support services to people fourteen to thirty years old, regardless of family income. Also offers workshops on Cherokee tribal heritage and history.

## CHILDREN'S DEFENSE FUND

25 E Street NW
Washington, DC 20001
(202) 628-8787
Holly Jackson

Seeks, through research, publications, public education, legislation, and other advocacy, to provide a strong and effective voice for children and to assure every child a healthy, fair, and safe start. Focuses on health care, family income, child support enforcement, child care, abuse, foster care, and violence prevention.

## CHILDREN'S EDITION

Urgent Action Network
Literacy Edition / Urgent Actions
Amnesty International
P.O. Box 1270
Nederland, CO 80466
(303) 440-0913
Ellen Moore, Program Coordinator

Children are encouraged to write letters protesting the mistreatment of victims by police or the military.

## CHILD WELFARE LEAGUE OF AMERICA

440 First Street NW, Suite 310
Washington, DC 20001
(202) 638-2952
David S. Liederman, Executive Director

Works with abused, neglected, and at-risk children, youth, and families by providing foster care, adoption, residential group care, child day care, and family preservation services and programs for pregnant and adolescent parents through nine hundred member agencies throughout the United States. Sponsors training, conferences, and workshops. Advocates for legislation for at-risk children and their families.

### CHRISTIAN SERVICE BRIGADE

P.O. Box 150
Wheaton, IL 60189
(708) 665-0630
E-mail: BrigadeCSB@aol.com

An evangelical Christian organization that offers leadership and fathering training and father-child programs for fathers and children ages two to seven through churches. Also available are meetings, special events, and camps for boys six to eighteen years old.

### CITY AT PEACE

P.O. Box 198
Washington, DC 20044
(202) 529-2828

Operating in Washington, D.C., City at Peace trains young people in peaceful conflict resolution through the performing arts. It encourages cross-cultural understanding and works to communicate the concerns and visions of young people to parents, teachers, and local and national leaders. Conducts workshops on nonviolent alternatives, theater, dance, and music.

### CITYTEAM

Youth Outreach
2302 Zanker Road
San Jose, CA 95131
(408) 232-5622
Lynda Haliburton

A nondenominational, nonprofit Christian service agency committed to meeting the physical, spiritual, and emotional needs of the poor in inner cities, including: the homeless; disadvantaged families; high-risk youths; single parents; women facing crisis pregnancy; and homeless, abused, and addicted women with children. Operates the Summer Urban Missionary in Training (SUMIT) Program, a nine-week internship of training and hands-on ministry experience for individuals who want to minister in an urban setting; a summer tutoring program; and youth outreach programs for children and youth from preschool through high school.

CLEAN AND SOBER STREETS

P.O. Box 77114
Washington, DC 20013
(202) 783-7343
Henry Pierce

A long-term residential drug and alcohol rehabilitation center for disadvantaged adults. In addition to substance-abuse treatment, the center operates a comprehensive program to provide residents with marketable skills.

CO-ETTE CLUB

2020 Chicago Boulevard
Detroit, MI 48206
(313) 867-0880
Mary-Agnes Miller Davis, Executive Sponsor

The Co-Ette Club operates mostly in the Detroit area and provides leadership training and community service for high school girls with emphasis on involvement in national and local charitable, civic, educational, and cultural causes. In addition to tutoring, the club reads and dramatizes stories to children in the Detroit public libraries. It cosponsors the Metro Detroit Teen Conference, which involves 250 ninth- and tenth-grade high school students from diverse ethnic, cultural, and socioeconomic backgrounds, who meet for group discussions and conferences in which they voice their concerns, hopes, and recommendations. The Co-Ette Club also raises money for the United Negro College Fund.

## COMMUNITY IMPACT PROGRAMS

Columbia University
204 Earl Hall
Mail Code 2010
New York, NY 10027
(212) 854-1492
Sonia Reese

• **Asian Youth Program** brings together student volunteers with a group of Asian children who have witnessed domestic violence and/or have been abused.

• **Barnard/Columbia Mentor Program** brings a group of middle school students to the Barnard Campus for tutoring and cultural enrichment. Volunteers are matched individually with students for one-hour tutoring sessions and then an hour for cultural-enrichment projects such as photography, poetry, writing, and drama, and other areas of student interest.

• **Big Brother / Big Sister** develops a regular and positive interaction with a strong and stable friend and mentor.

• **Community Youth Program** volunteers lead cultural and recreational trips to sites around New York City on Saturdays for kids from P.S. 145, a local elementary school.

• **East Harlem Tutorial Program** tutors elementary and middle school from throughout New York City at the EHTP center in East Harlem. Volunteers strive to establish in each child a sense of self-esteem and a love of learning through a consistent one-on-one tutoring relationship.

• **Mentor High School Extension** sponsors student volunteers to act as mentors to high school students. The mentors are matched carefully to ensure that the mentor and student share similar academic and personal interests. Mentors and students develop a contract outlining objectives and activities for the semester and organize group and recreational activities.

• **One-to-One Tutoring.** Volunteers are matched with neighborhood children as tutors for academic support. Volunteers tutor on Saturday mornings at Teacher's College.

• **P.S. 165 Tutoring.** Volunteers serve as teaching assistants at this neighborhood elementary school. Often because of overwhelming class sizes in schools, extra help is not available for students who may need more attention. Teachers are enthusiastic about the help and students respond positively to the volunteers.

• **TLC Play Group** brings together student volunteers with a group of nine homeless preschoolers at the Barnard College Toddler Center. Through creative play and interaction, these preschoolers have an opportunity to express themselves and develop early childhood skills that are crucial for learning.

• **LEARN and SERVE America: Higher Education Project.** Community Impact has been awarded a grant by the Corporation for National Service's Learn and Serve America: Higher Education Program for its national Empowerment Zone Education Success Project. This initiative will team CI with the Empowerment Zone in Upper Manhattan / Harlem. Community Impact will hire twenty-two AmeriCorps members to provide intergenerational education programming focusing on the entire family at schools and other community sites. Volunteers will mentor and tutor underachieving youth; teach, tutor, and counsel low-income adults in GED and ESL programs; and provide family literacy and citizenship workshops.

MAKING A DIFFERENCE

## COMMUNITY MUSIC CENTER

544 Capp Street
San Francisco, CA 94110
(415) 647-6015
Dr. Stephen Schapiro, Executive Director

In addition to instructional music programs, all of which are available to students who pay tuition based on a sliding scale, the center sponsors several other programs: Inner City Young Musicians Program recruits up to thirty inner-city students from middle schools to enroll in the Comprehensive Musicianship Program on full scholarship for intensive training, including private lessons, musicianship class, ensemble class, and performances; Children's Chorus is free to children eight to thirteen years old; Youth Jazz Ensemble is also free for teens with some musical background.

## COMMUNITY PARTNERSHIPS WITH YOUTH

2000 N. Wells Street
Fort Wayne, IN 46808
(219) 422-6493
Anne B. Hoover, Director/CEO

Provides training for adults who work with youths in schools, churches, and other organizations. Sponsors programs that teach youths how to be effective members of boards of directors and committees.

## COMPASS (COMMUNITY PROVIDERS OF ADOLESCENT SERVICES)

26 Sunnyside Street
Jamaica Plain, MA 02130
(617) 524-2333
David Manzo

Offers special education, intensive outreach and tracking, counseling, violence prevention, consulting, and enrichment services to over 7,000 children, adolescents, families, and organizations.

## CONGRESSIONAL AWARD

The Congressional Award Foundation
P.O. Box 77440
Washington, DC 20013
(202) 226-0130
Kendall S. Hartman, National Director

Youths fourteen to twenty-three years old challenge themselves to meet goals they've set to earn Congressional Awards by fulfilling national requirements in community service, personal development, physical fitness, and expedition activities.

## C.O.P. (COMMUNITY ORIENTED POLICING)

7101 Penn Avenue
Pittsburgh, PA 15208
(412) 244-4180
Lt. Dan Quinlan

A division of the Pittsburgh Police Department, C.O.P. maintains a force of over one hundred police officers, who, through the use of ministations and community-oriented involvement, work to establish a positive relationship and rapport with the neighborhoods to which they're assigned.

## CROSS BAR X YOUTH RANCH

2111 County Road 222
Durango, CO 81301
(970) 259-2716

E-mail: arnoldd@fortlewis.edu
Web site: www.fortlewis.edu/-danarno/crossbar/crossbarx.html

A Christ-centered camp for low-income children eight to eighteen years old. Activities include horseback riding, swimming, drama, backpacking, and mountain hiking.

## DIRECTION SPORTS

600 Wilshire Boulevard, Suite 320
Los Angeles, CA 90017
(213) 627-9861
Tulley N. Brown, Executive Director

Seeks to raise self-confidence, foster learning skills, and improve learning motivation in young people through peer-run academic and athletic programs. Operates in schools, after-school and recreation centers, YMCAs, housing projects, settlements, and youth detention camps in the United States and internationally.

## ERIC CLEARINGHOUSE ON URBAN EDUCATION

Teachers College Columbia University
Box 40
New York, NY 10027
(800) 601-4868

ERIC maintains a database of programs and research that examine how to teach young people to avoid violence altogether, or to keep conflicts from becoming violent by practicing conflict resolution; advocating crime prevention, gun violence education, life skills training, recreation programs, multi-intervention programs that use metal detectors to keep weapons out of schools and other public places, increased policing of schools and neighborhoods, and social and psychiatric services for at-risk youth.

ESTEEM TEAM

National Association for Female Executives
30 Irving Place
New York, NY 10003
(212) 477-2200
E-mail: nafe@interport.net
Angela Che

Women executives in a variety of fields serve as mentors to at-risk girls in New York, Connecticut, and Los Angeles.

FACING HISTORY AND OURSELVES

16 Hurd Road
Brookline, MA 02146
(617) 232-1595
Fran Colletti

A national education and teacher-training organization, its mission is to engage students of diverse backgrounds in an examination of racism, prejudice, and anti-Semitism in order to promote the development of a more humane and informed citizenry. By studying the historical development and lessons of the Holocaust and other examples of genocide, students make the essential connection between history and the moral choices they confront in their own lives.

THE FAMILY DEVELOPMENT PROGRAM

University of New Mexico
1128 University Boulevard NE
Albuquerque, NM 87131
(505) 277-6943
Edith Menning, Program Director

A nonprofit organization dedicated to empowering low-income families, children, and communities, FDP worked with professionals and low-income parents to develop Escuelita Alegre, a bilingual community preschool. Other FDP projects include the Baby Amigo Project / Community Sisters, which includes home visits to new families and a summer program for children. Materials available include a PBS video on FDP and other programs in New Mexico, and a video and narrative describing the development of Escuelita Alegre.

## FELLOWSHIP OF RECONCILIATION

521 N. Broadway
Nyack, NY 10960
(914) 358-4601
E-mail: fornati@igc.apc.org

Fellowship of Reconciliation's Peacemaker Training Institute for youth ages seventeen to twenty-five teaches active nonviolence to enact personal, social, and political change. The Institute holds intensive weeklong (and longer) training sessions across the country to diverse groups of youth. The emphasis is on teaching nonviolent strategies for conflict resolution, offering opportunities to meet experienced activists, and fostering leadership skills.

## FOOD FROM THE HOOD

Crenshaw High School
5010 11th Avenue
Los Angeles, CA 90043
(213) 295-4842
Aleyne Larner, Executive Director

Operates a student-owned natural product food company in an inner-city school.

FRESH AIR FUND

1040 Avenue of the Americas
New York, NY 10018
(800) 367-0003; (212) 221-0900
E-mail: freshair@freshair.org
Web site: www.freshair.org
Jenny Morgenthau, Executive Director

Provides free summer vacations to low-income New York City children. The fund owns five camps in upstate New York. Also sponsors the Friendly Town Program, which enables children to visit volunteer host families in rural and suburban communities. The children stay for two weeks or more in over three hundred Friendly Towns in thirteen states across the northeastern seaboard.

FUERZA JOVEN BILINGUAL NEWSPAPER

766 Valencia Street
San Francisco, CA 94110
(415) 252-5957
Bill Martinez

"Fuerza Joven" is a section of the bilingual newspaper *El Tecolote*. It is researched, written, produced, and distributed by a group of fifteen inner-city youth, who are coached and mentored by the newspaper's experienced writers. Also offers training in producing concerts and arts events. Participants learn journalism, writing, computer design, layout techniques, and most important, how to develop leadership roles.

GAY/LESBIAN/BISEXUAL YOUTH HOTLINE

The Indiana Youth Group
P.O. Box 20716
Indianapolis, IN 46220

(800) 347-TEEN; (317) 541-8726
Cindy Conley

The hotline is open year-round Friday and Saturday, 7:00 P.M. to 10:00 P.M., and offers peer counseling and support to gay, lesbian, and bisexual/sexuality-questioning youth. The goal is to reduce feelings of isolation and rejection, build self-esteem, and provide information to prevent high-risk sexual behavior and limit the spread of HIV infection and AIDS. Indiana Youth Group has ten chapters throughout Indiana and offers professional services, educational forums, social outlets, and an international pen pal network.

## THE GIRAFFE PROJECT

P.O. Box 759
Langley, WA 98260
(360) 221-7989
E-mail: giraffe@whidbey.com
Ann Medlock, President

Sponsors lectures and training in community action and offers recognition to people who "stick their necks out" to help others.

## GIRLS INCORPORATED

30 E. 33rd Street
New York, NY 10016
(212) 689-3700
Isabel C. Stewart, National Executive Director

A national nonprofit organization with 138 affiliates at over 900 sites, Girls Incorporated works with 350,000 girls ages six to eighteen to prevent adolescent pregnancy and child abuse; discourage alcohol, tobacco, and drug use; and encourage interest in science, math, technology, sports, and fitness. The AIDS/HIV Education Project provides information on AIDS/HIV and sexuality.

GOLDEN GATE COMMUNITY

1387 Oak Street
San Francisco, CA 94117
(415) 552-1700
Diane Hojsak

Serves inner-city at-risk families. Operates a day camp for children with AIDS.

GRAND PAIR PROGRAM

Roselle Public Library
40 S. Park
Roselle, IL 60172
(630) 529-1741
Elaine Thomas

Intergenerational reading program. Two people must decide to join as a pair; one must be ten years old or younger, and the other must be fifty years old or older, but the pair does not have to be related.

GUARDIAN ANGELS

982 E. 89th Street
Brooklyn, NY 11236
(212) 967-0808
Pete Kozo

Trained, unarmed volunteers patrol streets in over sixty-five American cities and some overseas locations as amateur crime fighters. About two-thirds of the members are between the ages of sixteen and twenty. In addition to the safety patrols, Guardian Angels operates a speakers bureau that sends representatives to schools to speak out against crime and violence. The organization also sponsors after-school clubs in New York City public schools that offer skills in communication and listening as alternatives to violence. Also offers an escort service for people traveling on the subways, buses, and streets.

## HABITAT FOR HUMANITY INTERNATIONAL

121 Habitat Street
Americus, GA 31709
(800) 334-3308

Habitat for Humanity is an international nonprofit, nongovernment Christian housing ministry, dedicated to the elimination of poverty housing. Home owners contribute hundreds of hours of "sweat equity" to the construction of their own homes, and then repay a long-term, no-profit, no-interest mortgage. Mortgage costs are kept low by the use of volunteer labor and by the donation of funds and building materials. Habitat for Humanity was founded in 1976 and to date has built more than 50,000 homes in fifty countries around the world.

## HEAL THE WORLD FOUNDATION

11111 Santa Monica Boulevard, Suite 370
Los Angeles, CA 90025

The Heal the World Foundation was founded by Michael Jackson to aid children and the environment. Its goals include providing medicine for children and fighting world hunger, drug and alcohol abuse, and child abuse. Heal the World works with established local and national organizations to share expertise and existing infrastructure in delivering needed services to disadvantaged children.

THE HIGH/SCOPE INSTITUTE FOR IDEAS

Adolescent Division
High/Scope Educational Research Foundation
600 N. River Street
Ypsilanti, MI 48198
(734) 485-2000
John Kenneth Weiss, Director

Aims to build a sense of community for teens through a four-week residential educational enrichment program. Participants from the United States and other countries learn about problem solving in the sciences and arts in a mutually supportive atmosphere. Also sponsors training and staff-development workshops for youth service professionals that offer strategies for implementing active and cooperative learning into camp, after-school, and summer programs.

IMPACT

Drug Use Is Life Abuse
P.O. Box 28
Santa Ana, CA 92702
(714) 647-4593

High school and college students who volunteer their time to help fight the "war on drugs and gangs" in their schools and communities. Their purpose is not to patrol their campuses but rather to make an impact on society and to eliminate drugs and teen violence by networking with today's youth through programs and activities that promote healthy lifestyles.

INDIAN YOUTH OF AMERICA

609 Badgerow Building
P.O. Box 2786
Sioux City, IA 51106

(712) 252-3230
Patricia Trudell Gordon, Executive Director

An organization committed to bettering the lives of Native American children. Seeks to build self-esteem and pride in Native American culture and looks for ways to help members advance their careers and grow personally and culturally. Operates an after-school program, provides outreach services such as counseling and casework, and sponsors a summer camping program.


INNER CITY OUTINGS

Sierra Club
85 Second Street, 2nd floor
San Francisco, CA 94105
(415) 977-5628; (415) 977-5568
E-mail: debra.asher@sierraclub.org
Web site: www.sierraclub.org
Debra Asher, Coordinator

A community outreach program that offers environmental educational and wilderness experiences for urban youth.


INNER CITY YOUTH SERVICES

901 E. Summit Hill Drive
Knoxville, TN 37915
(423) 524-7483
Mike Roach, Program Coordinator

A community outreach program staffed completely by volunteers that provides inner-city youth with recreational activities while strengthening spiritual values and stressing the importance of education. Sponsors a program that rewards students for educational achievement with all-expense-paid overnight trips.

## INTERNATIONAL GOOD TEMPLARS YOUTH
### FELLOWSHIP

International Organization of Good Templars, National Council
of the USA
2926 Cedar Avenue
Minneapolis, MN 55407
(612) 721-7606
Arlene Melton, National Director of Youth Work

Through national and international conferences, supports young
people in their efforts to abstain from alcohol and drugs.


## JACK AND JILL OF AMERICA

346 Commerce Street
Alexandria, VA 22314
(407) 843-6132
Barbara Newton, Executive Secretary

For children from two to eighteen years old and mothers who
are selected to be members by local chapters. Encourages community awareness and cultural, civic, recreational, and social growth.


## JAMES F. ACKERMAN CENTER FOR DEMOCRATIC
### CITIZENSHIP

Purdue University
4115 Liberal Arts and Education Building
West Lafayette, IN 47907
(317) 494-4755
Dr. Lynn Nelson, Director

Aims to provide programs and activities that develop young people's potential to become good citizens. Encourages student involvement in schools and communities. Selects twenty teachers on
the kindergarten through eighth-grade level to attend a two-week

summer institute that promotes citizenship education and service learning. At the end of the session, participants are provided with a $250 grant to implement programs in their schools.

JEWISH BIG BROTHER & BIG SISTER ASSOCIATION
OF GREATER BOSTON

333 Nahanton Street
Newton, MA 02159
(617) 965-7055
Patricia Schwartz

Provides Jewish mentors to Jewish children in the Boston area.

JOBS FOR AMERICA'S GRADUATES

1729 King Street, Suite 200
Alexandria, VA 22314
(703) 684-9479

Provides school-to-work transition and dropout-prevention programs to 30,000 at-risk and disadvantaged students in 550 high schools in twenty-six states.

JUNIOR AMERICAN CITIZENS COMMITTEE

Daughters of the American Revolution
1776 D Street NW
Washington, DC 20006
(202) 628-1776

A program for preschool- through high-school-age youth of all races, creeds, and economic backgrounds that emphasizes good citizenship and provides practical ideas for service in communities, homes, and schools.

## JUNIOR CIVITAN INTERNATIONAL

Civitan International
P.O. Box 130744
Birmingham, AL 35213
(800) CIVITAN; (205) 591-8910

A service club for middle school and high school students that encourages good citizenship, scholarship, respect for the law, and leadership development through various programs. Club members work with physically and mentally disabled individuals.

## JUNIOR OPTIMIST OCTAGON INTERNATIONAL

Optimist International
4494 Lindell Boulevard
St. Louis, MO 63108
(314) 371-6000
Steve Loos, Director

Student civic service organization that stresses leadership development, civic improvement, and participation in government and civic affairs.

## "JUST SAY NO" INTERNATIONAL

2000 Franklin Street, Suite 400
Oakland, CA 94612
(800) 258-2766; (510) 451-6666
Ivy Cohen, President

Concentrates on youth empowerment to help eight- to eighteen-year-olds find inner resources to cope with challenges and adversity and stay away from drugs. The Youth Power program is designed to emphasize their resiliency and encourages them to develop skills that will enable them to lead healthy, productive, and successful lives.

MAKING A DIFFERENCE

KEY CLUB INTERNATIONAL

Kiwanis International
3636 Woodview Trace
Indianapolis, IN 46268
(800) 549-2647
Leslie Murphy

An organization for high school students that offers leadership training and opportunities for service to schools and communities.

KEYS: KEMETIC EDUCATION FOR YOUNG SCHOLARS

P.O. Box 5881
Raleigh, NC 27650
(919) 515-1825

KEYS is a Rites-of-Passage program for African-American seventh- and eighth-grade students in the Wake County, North Carolina, area. The program focuses on the following topics:

• Cultural enrichment

• Womanhood and manhood training

• Life management skills

• Science and technology education

• Leadership training

These focus areas are designed to provide an understanding of positive and responsible adulthood, an African-centered worldview, and African and African-American history and culture. They also promote an awareness of gender roles and issues, stress knowledge of economic self-sufficiency, work to instill in youth a commitment to themselves and their community, and reinforce the importance of family and the larger African-American community.

196

Helpful Organizations

## KNIGHTS BOXING TEAM INTERNATIONAL

2350 Ventura Road SE
Smyrna, GA 30080
(770) 432-3632
Don Wade, Executive Director

A nonprofit amateur boxing charity. Team membership is offered to youths over twelve years old as an alternative to drugs, crime, gangs, violence, and suicide. Encourages clean living, health, and physical conditioning.

## KID-CARE

4504 Old Yale
Houston, TX 77018
(800) 566-0084

Kid-Care's philosophy is that education is the key to ending the cycle of poverty for the next generation. Believing that a hungry child can't learn, Kid-Care works to eradicate hunger in the Houston Metroplex through the first meals-on-wheels program targeted to children. Supported by corporate and individual donations, the organization also pursues ways to empower other communities to duplicate their efforts.

## LEGACY INTERNATIONAL

Route 4, Box 265
Bedford, VA 24523
(540) 297-5982
Mary Helmig, Recruitment Coordinator

An international organization that offers training to participants in twenty-five countries in cross-cultural understanding, global issues, leadership, community action, conflict resolution, and environmental awareness, and summer workshops and exchange programs. For youths eleven to eighteen years old and adults.

197

## LIONS YOUTH OUTREACH PROGRAM

Lions Clubs International
300 22nd Street
Oak Brook, IL 60523
(630) 571-5466, ext. 330
Denise Whistler, Youth Outreach Coordinator

Operates the Changing Tomorrow Today program, which encourages youth volunteerism as an alternative to violence, substance abuse, and gangs. Resources available are a teacher's guide, posters, and a video, *The Future Is Ours—So Now What?* Other programs sponsored by the Lions Clubs are Lions-Quest Skills for Growing, Skills for Adolescence, and Skills for Actions, which stress substance abuse and violence prevention and conflict resolution and are designed for presentation by schools.

## LITERACY VOLUNTEERS OF MASSACHUSETTS

15 Court Square, Room 540
Boston, MA 02108
(617) 367-1313
Roberta Soolman

Teaches reading to out-of-school youths, young people over sixteen years old, and adults.

## LITTLE FRIENDS FOR PEACE

4405 29th Street
Mount Rainier, MD 20712
(301) 927-5474
Mary Joan Park, Director

Teaches peacemaking skills to young children through churches, schools, and community organizations. Also offers day- and resident-camp programs and consultation and resources.

198

Helpful Organizations

LOYAL TEMPERANCE LEGION

National Woman's Christian Temperance Union
1730 Chicago Avenue
Evanston, IL 60201
(847) 864-1396
Natalie Wilson, National Executive Director

Sponsors youth groups that focus on abstinence to avoid drug and alcohol abuse. A catalog of materials on substance-abuse prevention is available from WCTU's Signal Press.

THE MULTI-CULTURAL EDUCATION CENTER

(A United Way Agency)
P.O. Box 1626
Palestine, TX 75802
(903) 729-3369; (903) 729-3488
Hylani Chan, Director

The Multi-Cultural Education Center works to meet the physical, mental, emotional, and spiritual needs of the residents in Anderson County by improving literacy and multicultural relationships; bridging the educational gap; providing training; and aiding families to find food, housing, jobs, counseling, medication, and exercise for the body and mind. Programs include tutoring, job placement, clothing, food, rent assistance, medical and dental services, summer programs for children five to fourteen years old, Spanish/English classes, emergency utility assistance, Red Cross training, counseling and guidance, transportation services, in-home services, blood pressure checks, income tax preparation services, referral services, and workshops in baby-sitting, sewing, and cooking.

NAACP YOUTH AND COLLEGE DIVISION

4805 Mount Hope Drive
Baltimore, MD 21215

199

(410) 358-8900
D'Andrea Lancelin

This division of the National Association for the Advancement of Colored People works to motivate and train its 60,000 youth members in six hundred youth councils, college chapters, and young adult councils to have an understanding of social issues, leadership, and organizational skills for community work.


NARCOTICS ANONYMOUS
World Service Office
P.O. Box 9999
Van Nuys, CA 91409
(818) 773-9999

Mutual support group for recovering addicts.


NATIONAL ASSOCIATION FOR THE EDUCATION OF YOUNG CHILDREN
1509 16th Street NW
Washington, DC 20036
(800) 424-2460; (202) 232-8777; (202) 328-1846

NAEYC is the nation's largest membership organization of early childhood professionals and others dedicated to improving the quality of services for young children and their families. The association's more than 88,500 members believe in the importance of the early years, birth through age eight—the critical years of development.


NATIONAL ASSOCIATION OF POLICE ATHLETIC LEAGUES
618 U.S. Highway 1, Suite 201
North Palm Beach, FL 33408

(407) 844-1823

L. B. Scott, President

Works to offer alternatives to violence and juvenile crime by fostering positive relationships between youth and police through over one hundred activities nationwide. Sponsors national boxing, basketball, baseball, and softball tournaments.

NATIONAL ASSOCIATION OF TEEN INSTITUTES

c/o C.D.C.

100 Billingsley Road

Charlotte, NC 28211

(704) 376-7447

John King, Administrator

Operates Teen Institutes that train adolescents in how to avoid substance abuse and encourage them to return to their communities to implement programs. Sponsors an annual national Teen Training Institute and a national conference.

NATIONAL ASSOCIATION OF YOUTH CLUBS

5808 16th Street NW

Washington, DC 20011

(202) 726-2044

Carole A. Early, Headquarters Secretary

Sponsored by the National Association of Colored Women's Clubs, these community-based clubs are for eight- to eighteen-year-olds. They encourage community service and sponsor talent, fashion, arts and crafts, and oratorical contests.

NATIONAL BLACK CHILD DEVELOPMENT INSTITUTE

1023 15th Street NW, Suite 600

Washington, DC 20005
(202) 387-1281
Evelyn K. Moore, Executive Director

Works to improve the quality of life for African-American children and youth by providing education to communities about ongoing issues and training individuals who work with these children.

## NATIONAL CENTER FOR YOUTH WITH DISABILITIES

University of Minnesota, Box 721
420 Delaware Street SE
Minneapolis, MN 55455
(612) 626-3014
E-mail: ncyd@gold.tc.umn.edu
Web site: www.peds.umn.edu.centers
Nancy Okinow, Executive Director

Sponsors seminars for parents, youth, and professionals from health, education, social services, and rehabilitation to educate these individuals about the needs of adolescents with chronic illnesses and disabilities.

## NATIONAL CHRIST CHILD SOCIETY

5101 Wisconsin Avenue NW, Suite 304
Washington, DC 20016
(202) 363-9516
Kathleen L. Gibbons, President

A volunteer nonprofit nondenominational organization that offers a variety of services to youths and children from disadvantaged backgrounds.

## NATIONAL COUNCIL OF LA RAZA

1111 19th Street NW, Suite 1000
Washington, DC 20036
(202) 785-1670
Ofelia Ardon-Jones

Works to improve the opportunities of Hispanic Americans through support of a network of over 20,000 groups, coalitions, and individuals. Emphasis is on youth school-to-work apprenticeship programs and alternative methods for teaching Hispanic youth. Sponsors an annual conference in July.

## NATIONAL CRIME PREVENTION COUNCIL

1700 K Street NW, 2nd floor
Washington, DC 20006
(202) 466-6272
Mari Nagorski, Executive Deputy Director

Seeks to create safer communities and reduce crime through youth training that directs young people's energies to build communities. Has developed a curriculum that pairs classroom experience with action projects that address actual crime problems. Provides training and technical aid to professionals in rural areas, inner-city public housing developments, and correctional facilities.

## NATIONAL EXCHANGE CLUB

3050 Central Avenue
Toledo, OH 43606
(800) XCHANGE; (419) 535-3232
Club and District Services Department

Sponsors the Excel Clubs, a program for high school students dedicated to improving their schools, communities, and country through volunteerism; the A.C.E. Award, which rewards at-risk high school students who demonstrate a dramatic change in attitude and performance and who become eligible for high school graduation; the Young Citizenship Award, which rewards those students who are good citizens at home and in their communities; and the National Youth of the Year Award, which presents a $10,000 college scholarship.

## NATIONAL FAMILY PARTNERSHIP

11159-B S. Towne Square
St. Louis, MO 63123
(314) 845-1933
Richard Evans, Executive Director

Promotes the formation of parent and youth groups with the purpose of preventing drug, tobacco, and alcohol abuse. Sponsors youth leadership-training seminars during an annual conference that teach about the harmful effects of tobacco, alcohol, and other drugs and discourages their use. Also shows the effects of advertising and provides instruction in peer pressure reversal. Participants are encouraged to return to their communities to use their newly learned skills and to conduct drug education presentations in elementary schools and youth groups.

## NATIONAL HELPERS NETWORK

245 Fifth Avenue, Suite 1705
New York, NY 10016
(800) 646-4623; (212) 679-2482
Alice L. Halsted, President

Young teens work with preschool and elementary school children cleaning up parks and streams in their communities. Training and technical assistance is available for individuals and organizations interested in developing similar programs, including Community Problem-Solvers, which provides steps for adults to help youths identify and solve problems in their communities.

## NATIONAL HONOR SOCIETY
## NATIONAL JUNIOR HONOR SOCIETY

National Association of Secondary School Principals
1904 Association Drive
Reston, VA 20191
(703) 860-0200
Rocco M. Marano, Director

Student members who excel in scholarship, leadership, character, and service are chosen by local chapters to provide service to their schools and communities, conduct peer tutoring programs, work at homeless shelters, and raise funds for charitable causes.

## NATIONAL INDIAN YOUTH COUNCIL

318 Elm Street SE
Albuquerque, NM 87102
(505) 247-2251
Norman Ration, Executive Director

Encourages social and economic development of Native American people. A program for recent high school graduates helps find employment opportunities. Also works to prevent the violation of civil rights.

## NATIONAL INDIAN YOUTH LEADERSHIP
## DEVELOPMENT PROJECT

325 Marguerite
P.O. Box 2140
Gallup, NM 87301

(505) 722-9176
McClellan Hall, Founder and Director

Emphasis is on creating opportunities for Native American youth to be positive influences in their communities. Sponsors leadership-training camps and comprehensive school- and community-based programs that work to develop leadership role models and include students and their parents. Participants are encouraged to return to their communities to share their leadership and service skills.

## NATIONAL NETWORK FOR YOUTH

1319 F Street NW, Suite 401
Washington, DC 20004
(202) 783-7949
Della M. Hughes, Executive Director

An organization that represents community-based, youth-serving agencies, its mandate is to ensure that young people grow up in safe environments, with positive values and neighborhood ties. Programs available include training for youth leaders, peer education, HIV/AIDS and drug-abuse prevention, and assistance in applying for grants. YOUTHNET is an online site on America Online.

## NATIONAL RESOURCE CENTER FOR YOUTH SERVICES

The University of Oklahoma College of Continuing Education
202 W. Eighth Street
Tulsa, OK 74119
(918) 585-2986
James M. Walker, Director

Sponsors Working with America's Youth, an annual national conference that trains child-welfare and youth-service professionals. Provides program models, training, and curriculum materials year-round. Works to improve the quality of life of at-risk youth and their families by raising the standards of human services.

## NATIONAL STUDENT CAMPAIGN AGAINST HUNGER AND HOMELESSNESS

11965 Venice Boulevard, #408
Los Angeles, CA 90066
(800) NO-HUNGR
E-mail: NSCAHH@aol.com
Katy McGiffin, Field Organizer

The nation's largest network of student activists against hunger and homelessness. High school and college students work to improve their own communities and raise money to combat world hunger through the annual Hunger Cleanup work-a-thon, a national conference, and Hunger and Homelessness Week. Also publishes manuals and a quarterly newsletter. NSCAHH is a joint venture of the student Public Interest Research Groups and USA for Africa.

## NATIONAL TOTS AND TEENS

P.O. Box 1517
Washington, DC 20013
(202) 723-5680
Gwendolyn H. Joe, Executive Secretary

The focus of this organization is the family, which it believes is most influential in teaching values and paving the way for youths ages three to eighteen to engage in positive pursuits and participate effectively in society. To achieve these goals, members work on community-service projects that contribute to the development of leadership skills.

## NATIONAL URBAN LEAGUE

Youth Services Department
120 Wall Street
New York, NY 10005
(212) 558-5470
Renita Carter, Programs Coordinator

Sponsors a variety of programs designed to help eliminate adolescent pregnancy, violence, and substance abuse. Seeks to enhance self-esteem by promoting community values, social responsibility, and the affirmation of the African-American cultural heritage. NULITES is a program for ten- to eighteen-year-olds that stresses community service, educational seminars, and leadership development. Sponsors an annual youth conference.

## NATIONAL YOUTH SPORTS PROGRAM

National Collegiate Athletic Association
6201 College Boulevard
Overland Park, KS 66211
(913) 339-1906
Rochelle Collins, Program Coordinator

Through a combined effort of the National Collegiate Athletic Association, the U.S. Department of Health and Human Services, and almost two hundred colleges and universities, disadvantaged youth are offered a five-week summer program at campuses across the country. The program includes instruction in sports, fitness, health, personal and social skills, alcohol- and drug-abuse prevention, and career and educational opportunities, and encourages the interaction of higher education institutions with their communities.

NEW BRUNSWICK URBAN ECOLOGY PROJECT

Department of Nutritional Sciences
Rutgers University
New Brunswick, NJ 08903
(732) 932-9224
E-mail: hamm@aesop.rutgers.edu
Web site: http://aesop.rutgers.edu/~nutrition/urbec.htm
Michael W. Hamm

Works with youth on food, environmental education, and community development programs.

NORTH AMERICAN YOUTH SPORT INSTITUTE

4895 Oak Garden Drive
Kernersville, NC 27284
(800) 767-4916; (910) 784-4926
E-mail: jackNAYSI@aol.com
Jack Hutslar

Provides technical assistance and training for youth leaders in fitness, recreation, education, sports, and health. Offers consultant services, leadership training programs, coaches' clinics, and teaching workshops, and acts as a clearinghouse for youth sports–related information. Sponsors "How to Coach" correspondence courses in basketball, baseball, bowling, football, soccer, and softball.

OPERATION OUTREACH USA

American Humane Education Society
350 S. Huntington Avenue
Boston, MA 02130
(617) 541-5095
Judith Golden, Executive Director

A national program that supports literacy, nonviolence, and character education for elementary school students. Free books and classroom materials are available.

## OUTWARD BOUND

National Headquarters
Route 9D, R2 Box 280
Garrison, NY 10524
(800) 243-8520; (914) 424-4000
Web site: www.outwardbound.org
Jack Bierwirth, President/CEO

Adventure-based education organization that maintains five schools and two urban centers. The programs are designed to develop self-esteem and self-confidence, leadership skills, a sense of teamwork, and an appreciation for the environment and community service.

## PARTNERS FOR YOUTH WITH DISABILITIES

1 Ashburton Place, Room 1305
Boston, MA 02108
(617) 727-7440
Joni Mullane

Mentoring program in Boston that pairs youth who have physical, sensory, and learning disabilities with adults with similar disabilities.

## PEACE EDUCATION FOUNDATION

1900 Biscayne Boulevard
Miami, FL 33132
(800) 749-8838; (305) 576-5075
John Mazzarella, President

Helpful Organizations

Provides training to teachers and youth group leaders in peaceful conflict resolution. Develops grade-level-specific teaching guides and videos stressing nonviolent alternatives, techniques for dealing with anger and frustration, the importance of respecting human differences, and positive interpersonal skills. Trains students to be peer mediators who help other students settle disputes.

PLUGGED IN LEARNING THROUGH TECHNOLOGY

1923 University Avenue
East Palo Alto, CA 94303
(650) 322-1134

Plugged In is a nonprofit community access and training center for computers and the Internet in East Palo Alto, California. Its mission is to bring the enormous technological resources of Silicon Valley to low-income youth and families.

PREPARE (PROTECTION AWARENESS RESPONSE EMPOWERMENT)

6219 N. Sheridan Road
Chicago, IL 60660
(800) 442-7273; (312) 338-4545

PrePARE teaches applied self-defense, empowering individuals to make personal safety choices in an emotionally supportive environment. Students practice both verbal and physical skills with a padded mock assistant. Training also includes verbal self-defense strategies practiced in role-playing scenarios.

PUBLIC/PRIVATE VENTURES

2005 Market Street, 9th floor
Philadelphia, PA 19103

(215) 557-4400
Gary Walker, President

A nonprofit corporation that works with schools, training organizations, community-based agencies, and businesses to develop strategies to achieve employment and self-sufficiency for youth.

RAINBOWS

1111 Tower Road
Schaumburg, IL 60173
(847) 310-1880
Suzy Yehl Marta, Founder and President

Trained volunteers work with elementary through high school students who are experiencing loss due to death or divorce. The twelve-week peer support program is designed to help children deal with their feelings of grief. Participating groups receive educational materials for use by religious and other youth groups.

R.E.A.D.S. (RETIREES EDUCATING AND ASSISTING
IN THE DEVELOPMENT OF STUDENTS)

Illinois Department on Aging
100 W. Randolph, Suite 10350
Chicago, IL 60601
(312) 814-2630

Retired individuals serve as volunteers in a reading program targeted to third graders or younger who are at risk of school failure.

RESCUE MISSION

120 Gifford Street
Syracuse, NY 13202

(315) 472-6251
Steve Tennant

Conducts a special summer ministry for inner-city children.

RIVERWOODS CHRISTIAN CENTER

35 W. 701 Riverwoods Lane
St. Charles, IL 60174
(630) 584-2222
Jessica Ricketts

Provides camping experiences for economically disadvantaged urban youths.

ROTARY INTERNATIONAL

1500 Sherman Avenue
One Rotary Center
Evanston, IL 60201
(847) 866-3000

Youth Leadership Awards are presented to participants chosen by local Rotary Clubs. Winners qualify for the program based on organizational and problem-solving skills, administrative aptitude, ability to get along with peers, and an affinity for public speaking. Workshops are held for youths from communities in the same areas, and include seminars on career exploration, leadership skills, conflict resolution, and how to be role models. Also sponsors Interact, an international program for fourteen- to eighteen-year-olds in eighty-six countries throughout the world that promotes leadership and integrity through school- and community-based service clubs.

SEARCH INSTITUTE

Thresher Square West
700 S. Third Street, Suite 210
Minneapolis, MN 55415
(800) 888-7828; (612) 376-8955
Dr. Peter L. Benson, President

Provides training and technical assistance to community organizations seeking to develop programs that emphasize healthy lifestyles and relationships and pro-social values for youth.

STUDENTS AGAINST DRIVING DRUNK

P.O. Box 800
Marlboro, MA 01752
(508) 481-3568
Marylou Vanzini, Project Coordinator

A student organization committed to fight teen drug abuse, drinking, and impaired driving. Sponsors community awareness and school-based programs and encourages the use of student-parent contracts and party guides.

SERTEEN CLUBS

Sertoma International
1912 E. Meyer Boulevard
Kansas City, MO 64132
(816) 333-8300
Leslie Freese, Director of International Sponsorships

Middle school and high school students work for a variety of community service projects.

## STREET SOLDIERS VIOLENCE PREVENTION PROGRAM

Omega Boys Club
P.O. Box 884463
San Francisco, CA 94188
(415) 826-8664

In March 1987, former public school teachers Jack Jacqua and Joseph Marshall founded the OBC to save the lives of youth lost to gangs, drugs, and crime. Believing that troubled youth were underdeveloped resources, they worked to redirect their lives. They subsequently proved that these young people could turn themselves around when eight of the first fifteen club members attended college. The OBC not only showed them alternatives to crime, but financed their college education and invested in their future. Since its inception, programs have evolved to respond to the needs of a rapidly growing family, both in the San Francisco Bay Area and around the country. The Street Soldiers Violence Prevention Program defines a "street soldier" as an individual who is committed to eliminating violence by reducing the risk factors that cause it. The program teaches youths to deal with anger and pain and to adopt new rules for living.

## STUDENTS FOR A DRUG-FREE AMERICA

P.O. Box 11948
Nashville, TN 37222
(615) 210-6562

An organization of drug-free college students.

## THIRD WORLD CENTER

Brown University
P.O. 1871
Providence, RI 02192

(401) 863-2120
Karen E. McLaurin-Chesson, Dean

Seeks to provide an environment for students of different ethnic minority groups to feel comfortable celebrating their heritage. Also works to expand the social awareness of students in relation to developments in Third World countries.

TEKOA

P.O. Box 90
Pilot, VA 24138
(540) 745-3887
Susan M. Duncan, Director

A nonprofit corporation that provides preventive services and possible out-of-home placement to youth and their families at-risk for delinquency, neglect, abuse, or family difficulties; resident treatment and special education for youth; assistance to youth, families, and other individuals with housing, economic, medical, and social needs; and educational and consulting services to other organizations and individuals who share a common purpose. *Tekoa* is a Native-American word that means "making camp."

TUTORING PLUS OF CAMBRIDGE

71 Cherry Street
Cambridge, MA 02139
(617) 547-7670
Diego Sanchez, Executive Director

Provides mentors and tutors to elementary through high school students.

## UNION GOSPEL MISSION

Youth Reach Out Center
3800 S. Othello
Seattle, WA 98118
(206) 725-2432
E-mail: Yroc@aol.com
Steve Bury, Director

Sponsors athletics, education, and other programs for youths six to eighteen years old. Also operates an inner-city ministry to after-school students and summer camps for elementary, middle, and high school students.

## UNITED CHILDREN'S FUND

700 13th Street NW, Suite 950
Washington, DC 20005
(202) 434-8917

A nonprofit general-assistance fund for educational programs and services for children, UCF supports educational programs concerning drug abuse, health, and fitness; presents festival events for children and the general public; and produces and distributes public service announcements regarding family-child relationships.

## VOICE OF CALVARY MINISTRIES

1655 St. Charles Street
Jackson, MS 39209
(601) 353-1635
Alexis Spencer-Byers

Community-development program for an inner-city African-American community. Provides family-practice health care, family and youth leadership and development, and housing services.

MAKING A DIFFERENCE

<u>VOLUNTEERS OF AMERICA</u>

3939 N. Causeway Boulevard, Suite 400
Metairie, LA 70002
(504) 835-3005
Valerie Maurice

Provides a diverse range of youth services in a variety of areas. Chapters are located throughout the United States.

<u>WAVE (WORK, ACHIEVEMENT, VALUES, AND
EDUCATION)</u>

501 School Street SW, Suite 600
Washington, DC 20024
(202) 484-0103
E-mail: SAVE4KIDS@aol.com

Targeted to young people facing barriers to success, WAVE provides educational opportunities, training, and motivation at over two hundred community, school, and workplace sites.

<u>WHEELER MISSION MINISTRIES / CAMP HUNT</u>

3208 E. Michigan Street
Indianapolis, IN 46201
(317) 687-3630
Cal Nelson

Operates a community center and summer camp for inner-city children four to nineteen years old.

<u>WILDWOOD RANCH</u>

4909 Brophy Road
Howell, MI 48843

(313) 965-3224
David Long

A summer camp for urban youth from the Detroit, Pontiac, and Flint, Michigan, areas.


WOMEN IN COMMUNITY SERVICE

1900 N. Beauregard Street, Suite 103
Alexandria, VA 22311
(703) 671-0500
Carole Gerlach, Director of Youth

Women in Community Service reduces the number of young women living in poverty by promoting self-reliance and economic independence. Provides mentors who work with women sixteen twenty-four years old on life planning, family stability, budget management, and other areas.


WOODCRAFT RANGERS

2111 Park Grove Avenue
Los Angeles, CA 90007
(213) 749-3031
Cathie Mostovoy, Executive Director

Operates after-school activities and camping programs for children in the Los Angeles area, particularly for those from disadvantaged backgrounds.


WORKING IN THE SCHOOLS

150 East Huron, Suite 900
Chicago, IL 60611
(312) 751-9487
Matt Pickering, Executive Director

MAKING A DIFFERENCE

A corps of over two hundred men and women (most of whom are retired businesspersons and professionals) volunteer in inner-city Chicago elementary schools, assisting teachers and working with the students.


WORLD OF DIFFERENCE INSTITUTE

Anti-Defamation League of B'nai B'rith
823 United Nations Plaza
New York, NY 10017
(212) 490-2525
Jim Smith

The ADL works to eliminate bigotry and discrimination through legal briefs, research studies and investigations, conferences, and educational efforts with schools and community and youth organizations. The World of Difference Institute targets its programs to youth groups, providing special training on recognizing and fighting prejudice.


YALE DEPARTMENT OF ATHLETICS COMMUNITY
OUTREACH PROGRAMS

P.O. Box 208216
New Haven, CT 06520
(203) 432-7413
E-mail: tim.ford@yale.edu
Web site: www.yale.edu.athletic
Tim Ford, Assistant Athletic Director

Sponsors programs that bring Yale athletics and athletes into the New Haven community, provides opportunities for community groups to attend athletic events and utilize Yale athletic facilities and fields, and provides opportunities for Yale athletes to become involved in community programs. A mentoring program pairs Yale athletes with New Haven middle school students to work on homework and spend time together. The Sport Clinic Program invites fifth-graders from an inner-city and a suburban school to Yale's Payne Whitney Gymnasium to participate in sport clinics conducted by Yale athletes and coaches. The program, which includes soccer, weight training, volleyball, lacrosse, and basketball, promotes friendship between inner-city and suburban children. A sports equipment drive solicits "wish lists" from area youth organizations and schools. Yale athletes serve as coaches for after-school basketball and soccer leagues designed to keep fifth- and sixth-graders off the streets and involved in sports. Yale athletes volunteer to assist with Little League baseball team clinics. The National Youth Sports Program, run in conjunction with the National Collegiate Athletic Association, offers training in sports skills, education enrichment, alcohol and drug prevention, and health and nutrition for disadvantaged children ten to sixteen years old.

## YMCA TEEN LEADERSHIP PROGRAMS

YMCA of the USA
101 N. Wacker Drive
Chicago, IL 60606
(800) USA-YMCA
Carmelita Gallo, Director of Community Resources

High school students participate in model state legislatures to gain a working knowledge of democratic procedures through a program called Youth and Government. Other programs available include Model United Nations, Black/Minority Achievers, Counselor-in-Training programs, and Earth Service Corps.

## YOUNG ADULT LIBRARY SERVICES ASSOCIATION

American Library Association
50 E. Huron Street
Chicago, IL 60611
(312) 280-4391

E-mail: YALSA@ALA.ORG

Julie A. Walker, Executive Director

Works with youth agencies to provide programs and activities that emphasize positive youth development.


## YOUTHBUILD USA

58 Day Street

P.O. Box 440322

Somerville, MA 02144

(617) 623-9900

Dorothy Stoneman, President

This organization invites youths ages sixteen to twenty-four who are unemployed and not attending school to construct and rehabilitate affordable housing in their own communities. Provides job training, education, and counseling. A high percentage of graduates are able to find construction-related jobs as a result of their experience. YouthBuild Coalition, the advocacy arm of YouthBuild USA, lobbies for legislation favorable to these programs.


## YOUTH FOR CHRIST / U.S.A.

P.O. Box 228822

Denver, CO 80222

(303) 843-9000

Roger Cross, Chief Executive Officer

Seeks to reach youth in middle and high schools, disadvantaged communities, inner cities, and juvenile institutions with the message of Christ. Offers opportunities for adolescents to participate in work projects in underdeveloped countries.

YOUTHFRIENDS

8701 Holmes
Kansas City, MO 64131
(816) 363-6014

Mentoring program that strives to create meaningful relationships for disadvantaged youths with caring adults.

YOUTH IN ACTION

1050 South Van Ness
San Francisco, CA 94110
(415) 920-7171
Tom Ahn

An urban conservation program, targeted to four middle schools
in transitional neighborhoods, that focuses on incentives to keep
students in school.

YOUTH LEADERSHIP INSTITUTE

944 Market Street, Suite 212
San Francisco, CA 94102
(415) 397-2256
Felipe Barragan

A violence-prevention program for high school students that
concentrates on helping at-risk youths make healthy decisions.

YOUTH MINISTRY OF THE UNION RESCUE MISSION

545 S. San Pedro Street
Los Angeles, CA 90013
(213) 347-6300
Teresa Escoto

MAKING A DIFFERENCE

Works to build relationships with youths in downtown Los Angeles through after-school and Saturday activities. Programs include mother-toddler groups, sports programs, camping experiences, holiday celebrations, and special events.

### YOUTHQUEST MINISTRIES

Center for Youth Ministry
c/o Liberty University
1971 University Boulevard
Lynchburg, VA 24502
(804) 582-2310
E-mail: jrandlet@liberty.edu

Sponsors mentoring programs for college and middle and high school students, including youth rallies, church internships, school assemblies, student conferences, camps, retreats, and cross-cultural ministry trips.

### YOUTH SERVICE AMERICA

1101 15th Street NW, Suite 200
Washington, DC 20005
(202) 296-2992
E-mail: info@YSA.org
Web site: www.servnet.org

Offers training, leadership-development programs, and technical assistance for community-service organizations.

### YOUTH SPECIALTIES

1224 Greenfield Drive
El Cajon, CA 92021
(619) 440-2333

Web site: www.youthspecialties.com
Tic Long, President

Holds an annual National Youth Workers Convention and the National Resource Seminars for Youth Workers.

YOUTH TO YOUTH INTERNATIONAL

700 Bryden Road
Columbus, OH 43215
(614) 224-4506
Lori Frantz and Jill Povoli, Directors

A community-based leadership program for middle and high school students that emphasizes drug prevention. Sponsors summer training conferences for adults and youth and offers a variety of "drug-free" T-shirts, buttons, and manuals.

YWCA OF THE USA

350 Fifth Avenue
New York, NY 10118
(212) 273-7800
Dr. Prema Mathai-Davis, National Executive Director

Membership is drawn from women of different backgrounds, faiths, and ages. (Men may join as associate members.) Emphasis is on empowerment for women and girls and the elimination of racism through peer education programs that encourage the development of self-esteem, decision-making, and adolescent pregnancy prevention.

ZUMIX

202 Maverick Street
East Boston, MA 02128

# MAKING A DIFFERENCE

(617) 568-9777
Madeleine Steczynski

An outreach organization targeted to disadvantaged neighbor-hood youths that sponsors a music mentoring program that matches adult musicians with young people; an audio/video/computer training program that prepares participants for entry into the workforce; and a streetwise drug prevention program. The name "Zumix" was coined by the kids.

# Index

# Index

# About the Authors

By night, ERIC DAVIS, JAMES MARTIN, and RANDY HOLCOMB are plain-clothes cops keeping the Chicago housing projects they grew up in safe. By day, they're the Slick Boys, who tour schools and towns across the country, rapping and telling their story. They have been named local heroes for their work in their communities and been commended nationally by media attention from NPR and *The Oprah Winfrey Show,* among many others.

LUCHINA FISHER writes for *People* magazine and is the winner of Chicago's Peter Lisagor Award for Excellence in Magazine Reporting. She lives in Chicago.